TRUTH
EXISTS

TRUTH EXISTS

FARA MARTIN

EQUIP PRESS
Colorado Springs

TRUTH
EXISTS

Copyright © 2019 and Fara Martin

All rights reserved. No part of this publication may be reproduced, distributed, or transmitted in any form or by any means, without prior written permission.

Published by Equip Press, Colorado Springs, CO

Unauthorized reproduction of this publication is prohibited. Used by permission. All rights reserved.

Scripture quotations marked (NASB) are taken from the New American Standard Bible® (NASB), copyright © 1960, 1962, 1963, 1968, 1971, 1972, 1973, 1975, 1977, 1995 by The Lockman Foundation, www.Lockman.org. Used by permission.

First Edition: 2019
Truth Exists / Fara Martin
Paperback ISBN: 978-1-951304-07-2
eBook ISBN: 978-1-951304-08-9

EQUIP PRESS
Colorado Springs

ENDORSEMENTS

"There is no more important journey than the journey to find out about God. The truth—as much as a human mind can comprehend it. Fara Martin has done us a great service in taking some of the very best research available and putting it in an accessible, compact form that an eager learner can digest. Key thoughts and ideas leap off the pages as resonating deeply with our mind, our experience, and our soul. I highly commend this resource to you!"

— **Mark Ashton,** *lead minister of Christ Community Church,*
Omaha, Nebraska

"In *Truth Exists*, Fara Martin has compiled a simple, yet comprehensive case for the truth of Christianity. In the spirit of a courtroom drama, Fara creatively weaves together a compelling masterpiece that is not only warm and inviting, but informative, well-grounded, and enlightening as well. *Truth Exists* is essential reading for anyone genuinely curious about ultimate truth—both for the convinced and the not-yet-convinced. It's an engaging read that you and your friends won't want to put down!"

— **Garry Poole,** *author and church outreach consultant*

"Here's a compelling compilation of evidence and arguments for the truth of Christianity, demonstrating once again that the facts of science and history point toward the reality that God exists and that Jesus is His unique Son. I encourage all spiritual seekers to seriously consider the implications of what Fara has put together."

— *New York Times* best-selling author **Lee Strobel**

www.truthexists.org

CONTENTS

	Acknowledgment	9
	Foreword	11
1.	What Is Truth?	15
2.	Can the Truth Be Known?	19
3.	Can the Truth Be Proven When You Believe It by Faith?	23
4.	Court Is in Session	27
5.	Is There Proof for Evolution?	29
6.	Are Variations Within a Species Proof for Evolution?	31
7.	Does Irreducible Complexity Disprove Evolution?	35
8.	Vestigial Structures	39
9.	What Is Life?	41
10.	Intelligent Design	45
11.	Does DNA Help or Hurt Evolution?	47
12.	Creationism	51
13.	Does Science Support the Bible?	53
14.	How Old Is the Universe?	59
15.	Did God Use Evolution to Create Everything?	67
16.	You're Only as Good as Your Word – Extra-Biblical Writings	69

17.	Do Prophecies Prove the Bible Is God's Word?	73
18.	Has the Bible Been Corrupted Over Time?	87
19.	The Dead Sea Scrolls	91
20.	New Testament Accuracy	95
21.	Are There Contradictions in the Bible?	99
22.	The Diversity of the Bible Is Evidence It Is God's Word	107
23.	Why Forgiveness Is an Expression of Love	113
24.	Good News	117
25.	If God Is Loving, Then Why Does He Allow So Much Suffering in the World?	123
26.	Is Morality Evidence for God?	131
27.	Closing Arguments	135
	Endnotes	140

ACKNOWLEDGMENT

To my husband, Andy, who is also my best friend. You have truly shown me what the love of Christ looks like in how you care for me. You also show me what seeking for the truth looks like. As a result, I not only learned how to ask the right questions, but have gained so much knowledge as I witnessed you teach others in their pursuit of truth as well. This book comes from watching and listening to you. What a blessing you are, Andy. Thank you for asking me to marry you.

FOREWORD

In my adult life I've struggled with back pain for decades, but it all hit a low point in 2015. As a result, I couldn't walk or even stand, which left me in bed for months. The pain medicine I had been taking up to that point caused ulcers, so I couldn't take any more medication and the pain was the worst I've ever felt. I had so much wrong with my spine that surgery wasn't a good option. But I slowly got better through years of physical therapy, which I still do to this day. Since I couldn't do anything but lie down while my back was healing, I wrote this book because my heart has always been burdened with the idea of truth and with the fact that many people are confused or deceived.

While talking with people about their beliefs, I realized how many of us don't even know why we have the beliefs that we do. Maybe that's due to never taking the time to think about where our beliefs come from. Maybe it's because we're too busy or distracted to take the time to slow down enough to realize this. Or maybe the topic of truth is too uncomfortable, so we avoid the issue altogether. Regardless of the reasons, my hope is each of you reading this will do yourself the favor of asking why you believe what you believe.

The painful experience I had with my back really tested my own beliefs. In fact, I'm at a point in my faith that I wouldn't be at if it wasn't for what I went through. I listened to well-meaning friends tell me everything's going to be okay and I'll soon get back to normal. But how did they know that? What if that wasn't true? I didn't want to hang my hopes on something that "may" happen, which pushed me to dig further into what I did know for sure.

And what I did know for sure was the love of God. Not being able to stand even to brush my teeth opened my eyes to all the ways God shows His love for me that I took for granted. And the simple gift of being able to stand was one of those ways. But not only that, I still had to face the possibility that I may never get back to where I used to be physically. I still had to face the possibility that I may have to live with severe pain for the rest of my life.

I accepted those possibilities and two unexpected things happened. First, and most important, was that even though I realized I may never get to where I wanted physically, it didn't matter since God became more important to me than any relief. And second, I grew in gratitude when I did begin to feel better and improve physically because I no longer "expected" it. You see, if you expect something and it never happens, you become disappointed. Maybe even angry. But if it happens when you don't expect it, you treasure it all the more.

God never promised me I would always be healthy, but He did promise me He would never leave me nor forsake me. Knowing something by faith is one thing, but to have that belief become an experienced reality is altogether different. And realizing that His presence is more precious to me than anything else is the greatest blessing of all.

I invite you to test your own beliefs by asking yourself this question, "If what I believe isn't true, do I want to know it?" I hope this book will give you some things to think about. Thank you for reading.

CHAPTER 1

WHAT IS TRUTH?

At one time or another, I think most people ask those big questions like "Why are we all here? What's the meaning of life? Does God really exist?" If you ask ten people what the meaning of life is, you will most likely get ten different answers. How do I know who's right? Or is there even a right answer?

So let's begin. What is truth? The dictionary says: truth is that which is true in accordance with fact or reality.[1]

Since truth is defined as being "in accordance with fact or reality," then that means truth is objective. This means truth is not influenced by personal feelings or opinions in considering or representing facts. Here's an example of an objective statement: 2 + 2 = 4. This is in accordance with fact and is true regardless of how I feel about it.

The opposite of objective is subjective, which means personal feelings, opinions, and prejudices are influential when considering a matter. Here's an example of a subjective statement: vanilla is the best ice cream flavor. This is subjective because my own personal opinion is the deciding factor. Therefore, it's not true. It's just my personal opinion.

Truth is not only objective, it also exists whether I'm aware of it or not. For example, a newborn baby has no idea that 2 + 2 = 4, but it's still true. Here's another example: people used to believe the Earth was flat and the sun rotated around the Earth. Obviously we now know neither of these beliefs is true. So let me ask this: since people used to believe these things, did that make them true? Of course not. Yet many people think that just because you believe something, then somehow that makes it true.

We hear the term "relative" quite often in regards to truth. People will say something like, "Well, that may be true for you but it's not my truth," or, "Live your own truth." But the notion that truth is "relative" is completely false. Truth is true for all people whether they know it, agree with it, or believe it. Truth doesn't change from one person to another either. We can't say, "What's true for you isn't true for me." When people make statements such as these, they aren't talking about objective truth, they are talking about subjective opinions.

Which brings me to two more characteristics of truth:

Truth is universal.

For example, $2 + 2 = 4$ is true no matter where you are in the world. It's true in a small village in Russia as well as in a large city in Australia.

Truth is also consistent: $2 + 2 = 4$ is true today, as well as it was true one thousand years ago, and it will remain true in the future.

To sum up, the three main characteristics of truth are that it is objective, it is universal, and it is consistent. So in the quest of seeking truthful answers to those big questions we all have, it's imperative to separate objective truth from subjective opinion, misguided assumptions, and wishful thinking. Everybody is indeed entitled to their own opinions, but opinions are not truth.

TRUTH EXISTS

CHAPTER 2

CAN THE TRUTH BE KNOWN?

Absolutely! In fact, we can know that 2 + 2 = 4 by testing it. If you know how to count, then you can test that statement by seeing if two oranges along with another two oranges really equal four oranges. Science has allowed us to discover many truths. For example, we know through experimentation that water boils at 212 degrees Fahrenheit. But let's take it a step further. How do you know when you were born? After all, you were too young to know what was happening, so how do you know your birthday is your actual birthday?

None of us know for sure when we were born since we were too young to remember. Because of this, we rely on what our birth certificate says. But how do we know what it says is true? We have to look to other things to give us enough assurance that what our birth certificate says is actual fact, such as the trustworthiness of the witnesses who were there when we were born—our parents, the doctor and nursing staff— along with trusting the hospital recorded the event accurately. So when we rely on the trustworthiness of the source of the information, we are believing it to be true "by faith."

Therefore, the truth can be known in two different ways:

1. Personal knowledge
This means we know something to be true because we have personally witnessed it.

2. By faith
This means we don't have personal knowledge, but we believe something to be true based on the reliability of the evidence given.

We all believe things to be true by faith every single day. Every time we go to the doctor and receive a prescription for medication, we end up taking the pills "by faith." We are trusting the doctor, whom we don't really know well, to diagnose us correctly. Then we are trusting the pharmacist, whom we don't know either, to fill the prescription with the right pills. Then we actually swallow the pills without knowing what's really in them, trusting they will help. We do all this by faith because we are relying on the trustworthiness of the people involved.

Which brings me to the next question...

CHAPTER 3

CAN THE TRUTH BE PROVEN WHEN YOU BELIEVE IT BY FAITH?

If we all know what it means to believe something by faith, like when we were born, then can we really prove that what we believe is actually true? What if the hospital recorded our birth wrong? What if our parents lied or were mistaken? How do we know for sure?

Let's apply this to evolution and creationism. These each make different claims as to how the universe came into existence. None of us have a personal knowledge of how the universe began since none of us were there to witness it. So whether you believe evolution or creationism, either belief is by faith. If we're believing by faith, then how can we know for sure how everything began?

Before we dig in, let's first define a few terms:

1. NATURALISM is a theory denying that an event or object has a supernatural significance; specifically: the doctrine that scientific laws are adequate to account for all phenomena.

2. MACROEVOLUTION is evolution that results in relatively large and complex changes (as in species formation).

3. MICROEVOLUTION is comparatively minor evolutionary changes involving the accumulation of variations in populations usually below the species level.

4. CREATIONISM is a doctrine or theory holding that matter, the various forms of life, and the world were created by God out of nothing and usually in the way described in Genesis.[2]

Note: There is a huge difference between macroevolution, which is what most people refer to when saying evolution, and microevolution. Microevolution has clearly been proven to occur. For example, there are wide variations of dogs, cats, fish, and even apples. This will be discussed further in chapter 6.

(For the remainder of this book whenever I use the term *evolution*, I will be referring to macroevolution.)

TRUTH EXISTS

CHAPTER 4

COURT IS IN SESSION

My goal is that you give serious thought as to why you believe what you believe. So many times we believe things just because they're popular or what we grew up believing. But are those solid reasons to believe in something? Please do yourself a favor and challenge the beliefs you have that are by faith. I won't exhaust every topic I cover in this book, but we will dig into them enough so that you can learn more.

So let's start the challenge...

Naturalism and creationism both have the same burden. Both make claims that have to be believed by faith. Naturalism claims that life began as a result of chemicals coming together to combust and form life. Then over millions of years, that life form changed through the process of evolution, resulting in the vast variety of life we see today. But where did the chemicals come from? Creationism claims that all life came from God, who created everything. So how do you go about making an intelligent choice as to what is true?

May I suggest you tackle this in the same way a jury decides a case in a courtroom? Imagine you were picked to be on a jury and you have to decide if the defendant is guilty or innocent. Since you weren't there to personally witness the crime that was committed, you have to listen to each side present their case, then weigh the evidence. You then make your decision that is based on the more likely scenario. You don't make your decision based on what is possible, but what is probable.

Juries do this every single day, so let's do the same here with naturalism and creationism. Let's start with the claims of naturalism. Is there proof one species can evolve into another species?

CHAPTER 5

IS THERE PROOF FOR EVOLUTION?

Charles Darwin had this to say concerning his theory of evolution in *On the Origin of Species*:

"The number of intermediate varieties, which have formerly existed on the earth [should] be truly enormous. Why then is not every geological formation and every stratum full of such intermediate links? Geology assuredly does not reveal any such finely graduated organic chain; and this, perhaps, is the most obvious and gravest objection which can be urged against my theory."[3]

If evolution is indeed true, then as Darwin pointed out, evidence of this would be truly enormous. On the one hand, we don't have fossil evidence that supports evolution since there still has not been found any "missing link" fossil proof. (*Missing link* is a term used that would apply to a fossil linking one species to another.) But on the other hand, we do have fossil evidence that supports creationism. This evidence is called the Cambrian explosion.

The Cambrian explosion is an event, as indicated by fossil records, in which most animal phyla appeared in a relatively short period of time that is too short to support evolution. According to www.allaboutscience.org, "...it is widely conceded that evolution of these organisms from unicellular precursors within such a short period of time is highly doubtful. It is surprising...that such a wide variety of fossilizable forms should appear at more or less the same time. There exists such a radical diversity that it becomes implausible that they shared a common ancestor."[4]

As Darwin said, if evolution is true, then there would be enormous fossil evidence to support it. Instead, the fossil records show that major groups of organisms originated separately from one another, rather than gradually over time.

"Large evolutionary innovations are not well understood. None has ever been observed, and we have no idea whether any may be in progress. There is no good fossil record of any."[5] Paul Wesson

CHAPTER 6

ARE VARIATIONS WITHIN A SPECIES PROOF FOR EVOLUTION?

There is much confusion when people use the word *evolution* when explaining the small variations within any given species. For example, Charles Darwin observed small variations in the beaks of finches while at the Galapagos Islands. People will often equate these minor changes that Darwin observed as proof for the major claims of evolution. These two things are different, and I'll explain why.

When Darwin observed the finches at the Galapagos Islands, the small changes he saw simply prove microevolution, which is small changes within a species. This is another way of saying there are variations within a species. But these small variations within a species in no way prove evolution, which is that one species can change into a completely different species over time. For example, the wide variety we see in humans doesn't prove we evolved from apes.

The finches that Darwin observed had different beak thicknesses, and this was due to the food cycle availability. The beaks changed in thickness according to how easy or difficult it was to get food. Their beaks were simply adapting to the demands of their environment. These adaptations, therefore, create variations within a species, which are examples of microevolution, not macroevolution.

Let's now take what Darwin observed and apply it to our own hands. We also experience adaptations in the thickness of our skin on our palms when we do more physical labor. The thicker skin areas are called calluses. This variation in our skin is due to how our skin can adapt to various tensions. This happens to me every fall when I rake the leaves in the yard. Species adapt to their environment all the time. But adapting is not the same as changing into a new species. Just because my skin can develop calluses doesn't mean my ancestors were alligators. This is why using what Darwin observed from the finches' beaks as proof for evolution is misleading. And it's vital that we are aware of this because people often use or confuse microevolution as proof for macroevolution.

There's an article from BBC News that claims "a population of finches on the Galapagos has been discovered in the process of becoming a new species."[6] But upon reading the article, no such discovery is evident. These scientists simply observed a male finch flying from far away, arriving at the Galapagos Islands, and then mating with a native finch. This mating resulted in offspring that these scientists say are a "new species."

Now how is that a new species? It's just one non-native finch coming to mate with a native finch. The offspring are still finches. We see examples of this all the time when a dog jumps the fence and goes to mate with a different breed of dog in another neighborhood. The puppies then have new characteristics representing both breeds; some characteristics are from the father's breed while others are from the mother's breed. But the puppies are still dogs; they are not a new species.

Professor Butlin says, "We tend not to argue about what defines a species anymore, because that doesn't get us anywhere."[7]

Is he kidding? Defining words is crucial to understanding truth and facts. If definitions no longer matter, then how can we communicate and understand what each other is saying? According to Professor Butlin, it just doesn't matter how we define things anymore. I disagree.

There is still no proof that one species can evolve, has evolved, or is evolving into a different species. In fact, the only proof we have is that one species continues to reproduce "after its own kind," just like the Bible says in Genesis chapter 1.[*]

---

[*] For an excellent article with more information on this topic, read "What Do the Finches Prove?" by Kyle Butt, M.Div., Apologetics Press, on http://www.apologeticspress.org/.

CHAPTER 7

DOES IRREDUCIBLE COMPLEXITY DISPROVE EVOLUTION?

Here's another quote from Charles Darwin in *On the Origin of Species*: "If it could be demonstrated that any complex organism existed which could not possibly have been formed by numerous, successive, slight modifications, my theory would absolutely break down."[8]

Michael Behe, a biomechanical researcher and professor at Lehigh University, claims he can indeed prove what Darwin said would destroy his theory of evolution. Behe's concept is called "irreducible complexity." An irreducibly complex system requires that every single component needs to be in place before it can function.

Behe uses the simple mousetrap as an example. A mousetrap has five components that are necessary in order for the mousetrap to work: the platform, the spring, the catch, the holding bar, and the hammer. All these components must be in place before it can work since it simply cannot work if one or more piece is missing. This challenges the theory of evolution since evolution is a gradual process in which slight modifications are produced for survival. Which means, evolution is a step-by-step process and cannot produce complex structures suddenly.[9]

So how does irreducible complexity challenge evolution?

Let's apply the mousetrap example to a single cell. As we saw with the mousetrap, all the components must be in place before it can function. The same goes for the cell. All the components of the cell must be in place before it can function, too. Therefore, the cell could not have evolved because it's an "all or nothing" type of thing.

Since evolution cannot produce complex structures suddenly, and since a cell is a complex structure, a cell could not have evolved. The cell, in other words, had to exist from the start, in its complete form. As Darwin admitted in his quote from above, his theory breaks down using Behe's concept.

Darwin's book *On the Origin of Species* came out in 1859. Since then, scientists have discovered a lot of information that Darwin simply did not know. As time goes on, researchers like Michael Behe greatly challenge Darwin's theory as new discoveries are made.

Also, if evolution was true, then think of the odds at which both a male and female of any creature would have to evolve at the same exact time in order for them to reproduce. Remember, your job as a juror is to decide what is probable, not what is possible. Is it really probable that at every stage of the evolution process, a male and female would happen to be at the same developmental stage and at the same place for mating to occur? Not only do we not have any fossil evidence of just one sex evolving from one species to another, but even if we did, we would need to times the odds by two for the other sex.

TRUTH EXISTS

CHAPTER 8

VESTIGIAL STRUCTURES

Remember studying all those pictures in your school science textbooks that taught evolution? Let's talk about some of those claims we learned as children. Some textbooks teach that "vestigial structures" give evidence for evolution.

A vestigial structure is an anatomical feature that no longer seems to have a purpose in the current form of an organism. Let's talk about two claims evolutionists make concerning these vestigial structures:

1. Textbooks teach that whales and snakes have vestigial hip bones and leg bones where legs may have once existed. Now it is true that they do have these tiny bones. But to say these bones are vestigial structures is false. In fact, these bones found in whales and snakes are necessary for mating purposes since they don't have any arms or legs. These bones aren't useless; they are extremely useful. To say otherwise is misleading.

2. What about the human tailbone? Some textbooks teach that the human tailbone is of no apparent use. *Heath Biology* from D. C. Heath and Company says: "The coccyx is a small bone at the end of the human vertebral column. It has no

present function and is thought to be the remainder of bones that once occupied the long tail of a tree-living ancestor."[10]

To say that the coccyx has no present function is also false. In fact, there are several muscles that attach to the tailbone, muscles you need for various important functions. And it also serves as an anchor when sitting. Just because humans don't have a tail doesn't mean we don't need our tailbone. If the human coccyx has no present function, as the *Heath Biology* textbook says, then try living without yours.

CHAPTER 9

WHAT IS LIFE?

We see reproduction of life all around us. But reproducing life is very different from creating life. For years, scientists have been trying to create life but have been unsuccessful. Back in the 1950s, two chemists named Urey and Miller studied the chemical reactions of gases yet never proved how life originated. In fact, it's created more problems for the claims of naturalism. Yet the school textbooks will say, "Swirling in the waters of the oceans is a bubbling broth of complex chemicals.

Some of them are carbohydrates, proteins and nucleic acids—the chemicals of life. However, the progress from a complex chemical soup to a living organism is very slow."[11]

That last sentence is taking a huge leap. It's assuming that just because there is a complex chemical soup, somehow that will slowly develop into a living organism. To make a statement like this is a subjective opinion. It is not based on fact.

For example, if you took a turtle and put it in a blender and turned on the blender, you would have all the chemicals needed to make a turtle, right? But having the right chemicals needed to make a turtle doesn't mean there will be life. Go ahead and try it. Blend up the turtle. You've got all the right material needed to make a turtle, and in the right amounts too. But just because you have the right chemicals in the right amounts doesn't mean you've created life. All you have is turtle soup. Having the right chemicals in the right amounts is a far cry from a living thing.

Paul Davies from the Australian Centre for Astrobiology stated, "Nobody knows how a mixture of lifeless chemicals spontaneously organized themselves into the first living cell."[12]

Evolutionist Alfred Fisher said, "Both the origin of life and the origin of the major groups of animals remain unknown."[13]

Life is much more than having the right chemicals. Life requires intelligence. It requires communication. This is where DNA comes in. There is undeniable intelligence contained in DNA. A good analogy for DNA (deoxyribonucleic acid) would be to compare it to our alphabet. Our alphabet has twenty-six letters that we use to combine in various ways to form words. We then use these words to communicate.

Let's say you were eating a bowl of alphabet cereal one morning and got up to go out of the kitchen for a few minutes only to come back to a message in your bowl saying, "Went to the store, love, Mom." You would know that your mom had been there and arranged those letters to communicate a message to you.

This is similar to how DNA works. DNA has four molecules, ATGC, called nucleotides. The order of these determines your unique genetic code. We use the same twenty-six letters of our alphabet to build words in order to communicate. DNA holds the genetic code to use the same twenty amino acids to build you. Just as there are various words made from the same twenty-six letters, there are various tissues made from the same amino acids. But not only that, your mom had enough intelligence to put the words in the proper order so that her message made sense to you. DNA also has the intelligence coded within it to put the proper tissues in order, which is why your eyes are on either side of your face and not on the bottom of your feet.

The use of the alphabet in arranging words and the use of DNA in arranging the blueprint to make you requires intelligence. You know that an intelligent mind (your mother) was responsible for arranging the letters in your cereal bowl to let you know she went to the store. So who is the one with the intelligent mind that's responsible for arranging the DNA to design you?

TRUTH EXISTS

CHAPTER 10

INTELLIGENT DESIGN

The four chemicals, ATGC, in the DNA molecule "function just like alphabetic characters in a written language or digital characters in a machine code. The DNA molecule is literally encoding information in alphabetic or digital form. And that's a hugely significant discovery, because what we know from experience is that information always comes from an intelligence, whether we're talking about hieroglyphic inscription or a paragraph in a book or a headline in a newspaper. If we trace information back to its source, we always come to a mind, not a material process. So the discovery that DNA codes information in a digital form points back to a prior intelligence."[14]

This is referred to as intelligent design.

When we look at a painting, we instinctively know there must be a painter. Or if you walk along a sandy beach and see a beautiful sandcastle, you also instinctively know the wind didn't make it. Someone had to have been there and taken the time to build it. Even when we look at the formation of George Washington's face, the first president of the United States, carved into the side of Mount Rushmore, we know there was an intelligent being that carved his face out of that rock. Why then don't evolutionists also instinctively know there must be an Intelligent Being that created the real George Washington?

You see, we don't have to personally see the artist who carved those presidents' faces because the artwork itself gives proof there was an artist. In the same way, we don't have to see God to know that creation had a Creator. DNA points to an Intelligent Designer in the same way a sandcastle points to an intelligent designer.

CHAPTER 11

DOES DNA HELP OR HURT EVOLUTION?

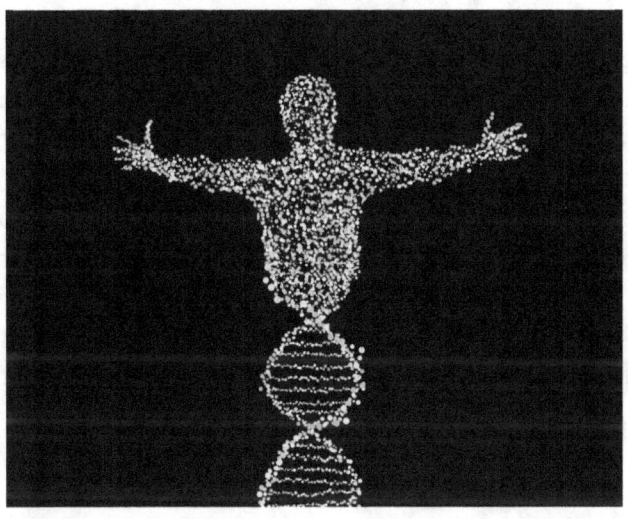

School textbooks have taught that humans share 98.5% of our genetic material with chimpanzees. This means there is a 1.5% difference between our genetic material. But now, the latest information shows there isn't a 1.5% difference as previously thought, but a 7.7% difference, with the gap growing more and more as we learn about DNA.

This poses a huge problem for the evolutionist since the original gap of a 1.5% difference represents 48,000,000 nucleotides and just a change of three nucleotides is fatal to an animal. So how can a change of 48,000,000 nucleotides be possible when only three proves fatal? And this data is applicable when they thought there was only a 1.5% difference. Now, they see there is a 7.7% difference.[15] Do you see the problem?[16]

To make matters worse, these findings are based on just a glimpse of the DNA researched. In fact, this result is based on about one million DNA out of the three billion that make up the human and chimp genomes. The more they study, the more differences they find.

DNA poses massive problems for the evolutionist. Because of this, the evolutionist will turn to all the things we have in common. And yes, there are many things we have in common with chimps and other animals even though the differences are staggering. But the textbooks will teach that the commonality means we all came from a common ancestor. Instead of saying we all came from a common ancestor, maybe we should be saying we all came from a common Intelligent Designer.

A man named Ernst Haeckel, born in 1834, made up the idea that the human embryo had gill slits. This has been proven false, yet it's still being taught from some textbooks. I actually remember learning this in grade school. Haeckel also confessed that "spontaneous generation must be true, not because it had been proven in the laboratory, but because otherwise it would be necessary to believe in a Creator."[17]

Why did Haeckel hate the idea of a Creator so much that he wasn't open to the idea that God exists and life comes from Him? Remember from chapter 1, we learned that one of the characteristics of truth is that it is objective. This means that our personal feelings cannot come into play when determining what is true. Haeckel's comment certainly doesn't line up with being objective, does it? For Haeckel, the idea of God was so offensive that he wasn't even open to that possibility. And if he wasn't open to that possibility, then was he really seeking truth?

To be sincerely open to truth means you must be open to wherever it leads you. Maybe for Haeckel, the thought of God being the Creator of life would mean God owns everything. And if God owns everything, then that means we are accountable to Him. Maybe the thought of this was too intrusive for him to be sincere in the pursuit of truth.

You see, I have no problem if you want to believe in naturalism. You have the right to believe what you want. But I'm writing about pursuing truth. So in the pursuit of truth, why is naturalism taught in school and not creationism? Naturalism is taught as if there's no other option. To only teach naturalism isn't education. It's indoctrination. Many universities today are pushing just one way to think, which is scary. The only way students can learn how to critically think is to have exposure to competing thoughts and ideas. So why not teach both naturalism and creationism, and let the students decide for themselves?

"In grammar school they taught me that a frog turning into a prince was a fairy tale. In the university they taught me that a frog turning into a prince was a fact."[18] Ron Carlson

CHAPTER 12

CREATIONISM

Let's move on to the claims of the biblical account, which is referred to as creationism. Right from the start, on the very first page of the Bible in Genesis chapter 1, it is written that God created all that there is. This account in Genesis would easily explain all the things evolution can't.

Creationism teaches that God created all the various species separately from one another, which is why we see evidence for that in the fossil records. It also explains why

DNA has intelligence coded right into it since it was created by an Intelligent Being. And it would explain where humans get their sense of morality from, all of which evolution has no explanation for.

Back in chapter 2, I wrote about learning truth through two different ways:

1. By personal knowledge

2. By faith

Whether you believe naturalism or creationism, either belief has to be by faith since none of us personally witnessed the beginning of all that exists. So is there anything we can look to that gives us good reason to believe the writings of Genesis are true? This is crucial because the Bible not only teaches creationism, it also teaches about where you will spend eternity by answering those big questions we all have about the meaning of life. So let's first look at science to see if it supports the Bible.

CHAPTER 13

DOES SCIENCE SUPPORT THE BIBLE?

Scientific observations throughout the years have actually verified the writings of the Bible. For example, the book of Job in the Old Testament was written thousands of years ago, yet remarkably, there are scientific facts written in this book before they were discovered through scientific observation.

Here are some examples:

*"He stretches out the north over empty space
And hangs the earth on nothing." (Job 26:7)*

Societies used to think the Earth was mounted somehow, like on pillars or something. Yet the truth that the Earth hangs on nothing by being suspended in space is recorded in Scripture long before science caught up to this fact.

Another verse in Job:

"When He imparted weight to the wind
And meted out the waters by measure."
(Job 28:25)

Science didn't discover the fact that air (wind) has weight until just a few hundred years ago, long after the book of Job was written. A man named Evangelista Torricelli discovered in 1643 that air can be weighed.

Here is a very recent discovery that was also recorded in the book of Job:

"Have you entered into the springs of the sea..."
(Job 38:16)

The "springs of the sea" depicted here in the book of Job weren't discovered until 1977. Scientists call these "springs of the sea" hydrothermal vents. Genesis 7:11 also refers to them during the Flood event, describing them as the fountains of the deep. The flood recorded in Genesis wasn't caused with rain only. The fountains of the deep refer to water beneath the Earth's surface that opened up, creating huge outpourings of water from below. This outpouring of water combined with rain is how the Earth flooded. Hydrothermal vents are still emitting water from under the Earth's surface into the oceans to this very day.[19]

More verses in Job:

"For He draws up the drops of water,
They distill rain from the mist,
Which the clouds pour down,
They drip upon man abundantly.
"Can anyone understand the spreading of the
clouds,
The thundering of His pavilion?
"Behold, He spreads His lightning about Him,
And He covers the depths of the sea."
(Job 36:27–30)

These verses are explaining evaporation and its cycle, which is what we now call the "hydrological cycle," which wasn't discovered until the seventeenth century.

Another book in the Old Testament describes yet another scientific fact:

Blowing toward the south,
Then turning toward the north,
The wind continues swirling along;
And on its circular courses the wind returns.
(Ecclesiastes 1:6)

Ecclesiastes 1:6 is talking about the jet stream, which was discovered by a meteorologist in the 1920s. Ecclesiastes was written way before this discovery was made.

And how about this verse in Isaiah:

It is He who sits above the circle of the earth.
(Isaiah 40:22)

How did the writer, Isaiah, know that the Earth is circular? Isaiah wasn't a scientist; he was a prophet. So how did he, and the other Old Testament writers, have scientific knowledge way before these truths were discovered? Could it be that the Bible really is the inspired Word of God? These verses that were written thousands of years ago give evidence that it is.

Or how about some of the medical knowledge we have today that wasn't available when Scripture was written? There was a practice that doctors used to perform called bloodletting. Doctors used to think that some illnesses could be cured by draining a person's blood. This procedure was actually performed on the first president of the United States, George Washington, which means the practice of bloodletting was fairly recent. In the Old Testament there's a verse that refers to the importance blood has for life:

"For the life of the flesh is in the blood..."
(Leviticus 17:11)

Many people died due to bloodletting, and this verse highlights the vital importance blood has for life, which, again, was written thousands of years before science caught up.

And what about the depiction of Jesus' death on the cross? Scripture states that when the Roman soldier stabbed Jesus in His side as He hung dead on the cross, both water and blood came out. It's recorded in the gospel of John:

But one of the soldiers pierced His side with a spear, and immediately blood and water came out. (John 19:34)

These verses are medically backed up by what we know about the human body today. There is evidence from Scripture that Jesus experienced hypovolemic shock as a result of being flogged. Prior to death, the sustained rapid heartbeat caused by hypovolemic shock also causes fluid to gather in the sack around the heart and lungs. This gathering of fluid in the membrane surrounding the heart is called pericardial effusion, and the fluid gathering around the lungs is called pleural effusion. According to the *Journal of the American Medical Association*, this explains why blood and water poured out from Jesus' side just as John recorded in his gospel, proving that Jesus died on the cross.[20]

The more we learn through science, the more science actually supports the accuracy, reliability, and authority of the Bible. Science doesn't discredit the Bible; it actually gives credence to it.

TRUTH EXISTS

CHAPTER 14

HOW OLD IS THE UNIVERSE?

Scientists use the Hubble Constant as a way of determining the age of the universe. The Hubble Constant is a calculation for how fast the universe is expanding. An expanding universe implies the universe has a definite age by retracing the action back to a time when everything in the cosmos was crammed together in an extremely dense, hot state. This is called the Big Bang Theory. The calculation of the universe's age using the Hubble Constant has been widely accepted to be 13.8 billion years.

However, this number has been recently disputed. A new study reveals the universe is expanding faster than previously thought, which means the universe is about a billion years younger.

Nobel laureate, Adam Riess, of the Space Telescope Science Institute in Baltimore, said, "The discrepancy suggests that there's something in the cosmological model that we're not understanding right."[21] And NASA astrophysicist John Mather, another Nobel winner, said this leaves two obvious options: "1. We're making mistakes we can't find yet. 2. Nature has something we can't find yet."[22] Now granted, on the surface, a billion years younger may not seem like much when the original thought was 13.8 billion years. But this actually is a startling discrepancy.

Another recent article says, "Astronomers are baffled by new measurements of the age of the universe which appear to suggest it's younger than some of the stars it contains."[23] Physicist Robert Matthews writes, "It's a riddle of cosmic proportions: how can the universe contain stars older than itself?"[24]

The takeaway is that scientists themselves admit they don't have all the answers, and will future discoveries challenge these current calculations even more?

There are also two beliefs concerning the age of the Earth. One belief is that the Earth is approximately 4.5 billion years old, while another belief is the Earth is only a few thousand years old. These two beliefs are commonly referred to as "Old Earth" and "Young Earth." I realize that this topic can sometimes be very divisive, but I'm not addressing this issue to create division. Since this book is about seeking truth, I simply want to share both sides so you, as a juror, can weigh the evidence.

I'll touch on just a few areas that challenge the belief that the Earth is billions of years old:

1. The Earth's Magnetic Field

Here's a striking discovery about the Earth's magnetic field. Evolution claims the Earth is billions of years old, but scientists have calculated the Earth to be much younger due to the rate its magnetic field is weakening.

They calculate the Earth being young because the rate at which the Earth's magnetic field is weakening indicates that the strength of the magnetic field would be too strong for the Earth to sustain life just a mere several thousand years ago. The magnetic field would be too hot for anything to survive.

Geophysicist David Stevenson at the California Institute of Technology says, "Right at this moment there is a problem with our understanding of Earth's core and it's something that's emerged only over the last year or two. The problem is a serious one. We do not know how the Earth's magnetic field has lasted for billions of years. We know that the Earth has had a magnetic field for most of its history. We don't know how the Earth did that. We have less of an understanding now than we previously thought we had a decade ago of how the Earth core has operated throughout history."[25]

2. The Oceans' Salt Content

Every year, the rivers and other sources of water dump water into our oceans. This water contains mineral salts. Over 450 million tons of sodium goes into our oceans every year from this water. Only 27% of this sodium manages to get out of the oceans, while the remainder accumulates year after year. As of this writing, the oceans contain 3.6% sodium. If the Earth is billions of years old, the salt content of the oceans would be much higher than it is now.[26]

3. The Geologic Column

Have you heard of the geologic column? Maybe you remember it from your school days. Here's an example of it:

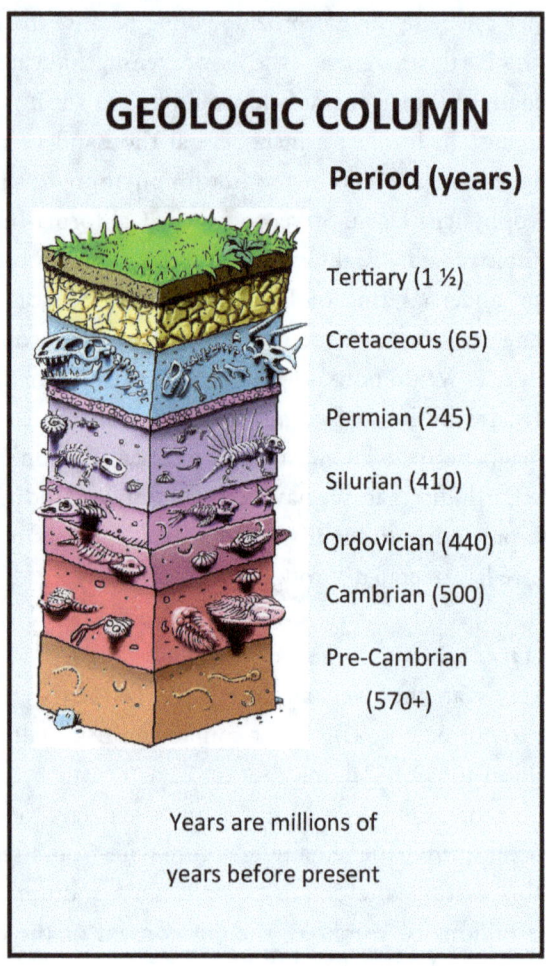

Now, it's true that the Earth has layers, but science textbooks have added these fossils to the layers in an attempt to show evolution by attaching dates to the various layers. But is this really true? How do they know the age of each rock layer?

According to the geologists, they can tell the age of the rock layer by how old the fossils are in that layer. These are called "index fossils." But then they will tell you they can tell the age of a fossil by what rock layer it's found in. So, on the one hand, they can tell the age of the layer by how old the fossil is, and on the other hand they can tell how old the fossil is by what layer it's in. Wait a minute, isn't this circular reasoning? The whole premise of the geologic column is false. You can't say the rocks are dated by the fossils and at the same time say the fossils are dated by the rocks.

"The intelligent layman has long suspected circular reasoning in the use of rocks to date fossils and fossils to date rocks. The geologist has never bothered to think of a good reply, feeling the explanations are not worth the trouble as long as the work brings results." (J. E. O'Rourke, *American Journal of Science* 1976)[27]

"It cannot be denied that from a strictly philosophical standpoint geologists are here arguing in a circle. The succession of organisms has been determined by a study of their remains embedded in the rocks, and the relative ages of the rocks are determined by the remains of organisms that they contain." (R. H. Rastall, "Geology," *Encyclopaedia Britannica*, vol. 10, 1949)[28]

"Paleontologists cannot operate this way. There is no way simply to look at a fossil and say how old it is unless you know the age of the rocks it comes from. And this poses something of a problem: if we date the rocks by their fossils, how can we then turn around and talk about patterns of evolutionary change through time in the fossil record?" (Evolutionist Niles Eldredge, *Time Frames: The Rethinking of Darwinian Evolution and the Theory of Punctuated Equilibria*)[29]

Also, we can't know for sure that the deeper fossils found in the deepest layers of rock are the oldest, while the shallow fossils are the youngest. This would only be true if the water present during that time was still. But if the water was moving, like in violent floodwaters, then the animals and settling of the soil would get all jumbled up, ending in chaotic settling. We simply can't know for sure the deepest fossils are the oldest.

4. Canyons

It's amazing to me how two people can look at the same thing and come up with two completely different explanations. Well, you guessed it, there are different interpretations of how the different layers of the Earth's crust were formed. Some say these rock layers give us a picture of the billions of years of history of the Earth, while others say these rock layers were formed during the catastrophic flood recorded in the Bible in Genesis chapter 7. So what's true?

We have evidence that canyons can easily be formed in short time periods, given enough water. For example, a smaller canyon named Burlingame Canyon, near Walla Walla, Washington, USA, was formed in six days.

Also, as we look at the layers in the Grand Canyon, we have to ask, "Why aren't there any erosion marks between the layers? And if the layers are from different ages, then why aren't there any layers of soil between the layers of rock?" After all, if these layers were formed over billions of years, there would be rain during that time, so of course there should be evidence of erosion and soil settling between the layers. So why don't we have that evidence? Instead, the layers are stacked like pancakes, which is more indicative of it happening rapidly. The idea that canyons need long periods of time to develop is false, as we have evidence to the contrary.[30]

5. Were Humans Created at a Specific Time?

Since none of us were there when the first man and woman came into existence, we have to rely on someone who was there. Since the Bible tells us that God created the first man and woman, then He was there. Jesus makes a very interesting statement concerning when the first man and woman were created while He was answering a question about divorce:

*"Have you not read that He who created them
from the beginning made them male and female..."
(Matthew 19:4)*

From this verse, Jesus not only validates the creation account in Genesis but also states when human beings were first created: "from the beginning." He did not say humans were created thousands, millions, or billions of years after the beginning. This is important since it means not only were humans created separately as a specific act (rather than slowly evolving over time), but they were created at a specific time, "from the beginning."

These are just a few examples that point to the claim the Earth is much younger than billions of years. Yet let me be clear. In no way am I stating that in order to be a Christian you have to believe in a young Earth. How you respond to the good news of Jesus Christ will determine whether or not you are a Christian, not how old you think the universe or the Earth is.

CHAPTER 15

DID GOD USE EVOLUTION TO CREATE EVERYTHING?

Evolution says that life slowly improves over time and that these evolutionary changes happen for some kind of advantage. Whereas the Bible says everything started out perfect and is slowly deteriorating over time due to death entering the world as a result of Adam's sin. This is why Genesis records people living hundreds of years when they were first created, then due to the Flood and how the Earth dramatically changed, the life span decreased. Test it for yourself and examine the state of the Earth today: does it seem to be improving or deteriorating?

Teachings that say God used evolution to create everything are at odds with the Bible since evolution depends on death for organisms to slowly change. Evolution states that life slowly evolves over time by repeated "life/death cycles" as organisms change into various forms of life. However, the Bible states that death didn't even enter creation until after Adam sinned. How could humans have evolved over time through many cycles of life and death, when death didn't even occur until after humans already existed?

The Bible says man brought death into the world, while evolution says death brought man into the world. God could not have used evolution to create everything because creationism and evolution are at odds not only scientifically but also theologically.

CHAPTER 16

YOU'RE ONLY AS GOOD AS YOUR WORD – EXTRA-BIBLICAL WRITINGS

Have you ever heard the statement "You're only as good as your word"? It means that if your word can't be trusted, then you can't be trusted. Since the Bible makes claims that go beyond creationism, then I think it's vital to look at the trustworthiness of the Bible as a whole.

What's one way we can check the truthfulness of a person's words? Well, we can always check what they say to see if other sources corroborate their words. For example, if all the news channels were covering the same story, but they all had different facts, how would we know which news channel was right? But if all the news channels had the same facts, then it lends credibility to the truthfulness of the story.

The same goes with the Bible. The Bible claims to be the very Word of God, so, are there other sources we can look to that would corroborate the stories in the Bible?

Below is a list of seventeen different statements. As you read them, you would think these statements all came from the Bible. Here they are:

1. Jesus was born and lived in Palestine.
2. He was born, supposedly, to a virgin and had an earthly father who was a carpenter.
3. He was a teacher who taught that by repentance and belief, all followers would become brothers and sisters.
4. He led the Jews away from their beliefs.
5. He was a wise man who claimed to be God and the Messiah.
6. He had unusual magical powers and performed miraculous deeds.
7. He healed the lame.
8. He accurately predicted the future.
9. He was persecuted by the Jews for what he said, betrayed by Judah Iskarioto.
10. He was beaten with rods, forced to drink vinegar and wear a crown of thorns, and crucified on the eve of Passover.
11. His crucifixion occurred under the direction of Pontius Pilate, during the time of Tiberius.
12. On the day of his crucifixion, the sky grew dark and there was an earthquake. Afterward, he was buried in a tomb, and the tomb was later found to be empty.
13. He appeared to his disciples resurrected from the grave and showed them his wounds.
14. These disciples then told others that Jesus was resurrected and ascended into heaven.

15. Jesus' disciples and followers upheld a high moral code. One of them was named Matthai.
16. The disciples were also persecuted for their faith but were martyred without changing their claims.
17. They met regularly to worship Jesus, even after his death.

Well, as it so happens, none of these statements came from the Bible. Amazingly, there are very few manuscripts of any text written during Jesus' time. In fact, historians of this era simply didn't write much about religious figures. These seventeen statements all came from these sources I will list below that are either from extra-biblical historical documents or historians. Here they are:

Thallus (52 AD)
Pliny the Younger (61-113 AD)
Suetonius (69-140 AD)
Tacitus (56-120 AD)
Mara Bar-Serapion (70 AD)
Phlegon (80-140 AD)
Lucian of Samosata (115-200 AD)
Celsus (175 AD)
Josephus (37-101 AD)
Jewish Talmud (400-700 AD)
The Toledot Yeshu (1000 AD)[31]

Another thing that gives credence to the biblical accounts is all the historical dates, places, and people that the Bible records. For example, many people think the stories of Noah and the Flood or Jonah and the fish are nothing more than myths. But myths don't bother with specific details. Why? Because details can be verified to see if they are factual or not. Instead, myths use words like "once upon a time in a far-off land."

So not only does the Bible itself support its reliability by giving detailed facts to its historical stories, but sources outside the Bible corroborate claims made by the Bible as well. These extra-biblical writings are very consistent with what the Bible says.

The same goes for Bible prophecies. A prophecy proves to be true when it actually happens. Living today gives us a huge advantage as we can look back through history to see if certain prophecies came true. So in the next chapter, we'll dig into some of the prophecies to see if they did indeed come to pass.

CHAPTER 17

DO PROPHECIES PROVE THE BIBLE IS GOD'S WORD?

The Bible is filled with prophecies, in both the Old and New Testaments. It's amazing how accurate and detailed these prophecies are, which give them even more credibility when they come true. Since there are so many prophecies I'll just give a few examples, starting with some historical prophecies, then moving on to some messianic prophecies.

In the Old Testament, the book of Daniel gives us many prophecies concerning various rises and falls of different kings and kingdoms. We can easily look back throughout history to see if these prophecies came true, which they did in spectacular detail. In fact, these prophecies are so accurate that some people have denied the book of Daniel was written before these prophecies came about since there is no explanation for their validity other than this truly being the written Word of God.

For example, the prophecies in Daniel chapter 8 unfolded throughout history as we can look back to see how the images in this chapter line up and describe the specific human beings who matched and carried out these prophecies. I'll let you read the verses first and then we can see how history reveals these images:

Then I lifted my eyes and looked, and behold, a ram which had two horns was standing in front of the canal. Now the two horns were long, but one was longer than the other, with the longer one coming up last. I saw the ram butting westward, northward, and southward, and no other beasts could stand before him nor was there anyone to rescue from his power, but he did as he pleased and magnified himself.
While I was observing, behold, a male goat was coming from the west over the surface of the whole earth without touching the ground; and the goat had a conspicuous horn between his eyes. He came up to the ram that had the two horns, which I had seen standing in front of the canal, and rushed at him in his mighty wrath. I saw him come beside the ram, and he was enraged at him; and he struck the ram and shattered his two horns, and the ram had no strength to withstand him. So he hurled him to the ground and trampled on him, and there was none to rescue the ram from his power. Then the male goat magnified himself exceedingly. But as soon as he was mighty, the large horn was broken; and in its place there came up four conspicuous horns toward the four winds of heaven. (Daniel 8:3–8)

History can explain the imagery in these verses. The ram described in Daniel 8:3 symbolizes the Medo-Persian Empire, with the two horns representing the two entities (Medes and the Persians) merging into one. The male goat in verse 5 represents Greece, with its horn being Alexander the Great. Verse 5 describes this goat as moving so swiftly that it doesn't even touch the ground. This pictures how Alexander's army of thirty-five thousand moved with great speed as they conquered the Medo-Persian Empire and formed the Greco-Macedonian Empire. The death of Alexander is then described as a broken horn in verse 8. After his death, the four horns represent Alexander's kingdom being divided into four regions, with four of Alexander's generals taking over: Ptolemy was king of Egypt, Cassander was king of Macedonia and Greece, Lysimachus was king of Asia, and Seleucus was king of Syria.

History records these events taking place, so it's easy to verify. But what's so amazing is the detail that is recorded in Daniel, such detail that there can be no mistake this is truly prophecy from God as recorded by Daniel years before any of this took place.

Another prophecy in Daniel, chapter 7, describes four world-ruling kingdoms, in which these kingdoms will impact God's people until God's kingdom is ultimately established. The first beast that Daniel saw in his vision in Daniel 7:4 is described as a lion; then he sees a bear, then a leopard, followed by a fourth beast that is different from the others. As we look back through history we can see that the lion represents Babylon, the bear represents Medo-Persia, the leopard represents Greece, while the fourth beast points to the Roman Empire.

As history proves, the Roman Empire did indeed conquer Syria and Palestine, and as Daniel's prophecies predicted, the Roman Empire was greater, stronger, and lasted longer than the previous empires. The Roman Empire eventually fell apart, yet continued to live on in a divided status (Europe), and will be revived and regain its strength as Jesus' Second Coming nears.

Here is another amazingly precise prophecy:

"Then he will return to his land with much plunder; but his heart will be set against the holy covenant, and he will take action and then return to his own land.
"At the appointed time he will return and come into the South, but this last time it will not turn out the way it did before. For ships of Kittim will come against him; therefore he will be disheartened and will return and become enraged at the holy covenant and take action; so he will come back and show regard for those who forsake the holy covenant. Forces from him will arise, desecrate the sanctuary fortress, and do away with the regular sacrifice. And they will set up the abomination of desolation."
(Daniel 11:28–31)

These verses came true when Antiochus halted all Jewish worship, banning circumcision and daily sacrifices in Israel's temple, and sacrificed a pig on the altar. What's also important to note is that Jesus referred to this "abomination of desolation" when He said this would also happen under the rule of the final Antichrist (Matthew 24:15).

So Jesus not only validates Daniel's prophecy but uses it to point to a future prophecy. And since the past prophecies came about with such detailed certainty, this gives us good reason to believe the prophecies that are still for the future.

Now concerning the messianic prophecies. It is only through Jesus' life, death, and resurrection do we see these prophecies come true. The first I'll address concerns the Passover. In the Old Testament, God went into great detail concerning this special feast day. In Exodus chapter 12, God instructed the Israelites how they were to celebrate the Passover since it marked what took place in Egypt as God delivered them from the bondage of slavery. This tradition was unique since it was the only one that was first celebrated before they left Egypt. All other special feast days on the Jewish calendar were given afterwards, therefore marking the Passover as the day of redemption from Egypt.

But here is a very interesting detail. In Exodus 12:46, God gives specific instructions about how the Israelites were to eat the Passover lamb,

> *"It is to be eaten in a single house; you are not to bring forth any of the flesh outside of the house, nor are you to break any bone of it."*

Later, in Numbers chapter 9 verse 12, God reiterates the command of not breaking any of its bones:

"They shall leave none of it until morning, nor break a bone of it; according to all the statute of the Passover they shall observe it."

This is prophetic because Jesus is also referred to as the Lamb of God since He offered Himself as the sacrifice that would deliver anyone who trusts in Him from their bondage to sin. And just as the Passover lamb was to not have any bones broken, this was fulfilled through Jesus since He also never had any bones broken.

We read about this in the gospel of John when Jesus, along with two others, was hanging on the cross. You see, when someone was crucified on a cross, the weight of their body wouldn't allow them to breathe since their arms were pulled out to their sides. So in order to breathe, they had to push up on their feet to try and get air. This had to be done continually with each breath, which was excruciating since their feet were also nailed to the cross. If the soldiers wanted to speed up their death, they would break their legs, which caused them to suffocate since they could no longer breathe.

Here's the account as recorded in John 19:31-33:

Then the Jews, because it was the day of preparation, so that the bodies would not remain on the cross on the Sabbath (for that Sabbath was a high day), asked Pilate that their legs might be broken, and that they might be taken away. So the soldiers came, and broke the legs of the first man and of the other who was crucified with Him; but coming to Jesus, when they saw that He was already dead, they did not break His legs.

Not only does Jesus fulfill this prophecy from the Old Testament concerning this detail, but it also shows how He is the true Passover Lamb as He is offered up to deliver people from their sins.

Other prophecies concerning the Messiah are found in Isaiah chapter 53. This chapter is filled with language of substitution in that the Servant described in this chapter is innocent yet suffered chastisement from God to provide our peace with God. Later, in the New Testament, we see these prophecies fulfilled in detail through the substitutionary death of Jesus on the cross, as He took God's wrath for sin upon Himself on behalf of sinners.

I will give only a few here even though there are many others:

Isaiah 53:1–12
The Suffering Servant

Who has believed our message?
And to whom has the arm of the Lord been revealed?

*² For He grew up before Him like a tender shoot,
And like a root out of parched ground;
He has no stately form or majesty
That we should look upon Him,
Nor appearance that we should be attracted to
Him.*

(Prophecy fulfilled in Matthew 13:55–57, John 1:45–46)

*³ He was despised and forsaken of men,
A man of sorrows and acquainted with grief;
And like one from whom men hide their face
He was despised, and we did not esteem Him.*

(Prophecy fulfilled in Luke 4:16–30, John 8:48, John 19:21)

*⁴ Surely our griefs He Himself bore,
And our sorrows He carried;
Yet we ourselves esteemed Him stricken,
Smitten of God, and afflicted.*

(Prophecy fulfilled in Colossians 2:14)

*⁵ But He was pierced through for our
transgressions,
He was crushed for our iniquities;
The chastening for our well-being fell upon Him,
And by His scourging we are healed.*

(Prophecy fulfilled in 1 Peter 2:24)

⁶ All of us like sheep have gone astray,
Each of us has turned to his own way;
But the Lord has caused the iniquity of us all
To fall on Him.

(Prophecy fulfilled in Acts 2:23)

⁷ He was oppressed and He was afflicted,
Yet He did not open His mouth;
Like a lamb that is led to slaughter,
And like a sheep that is silent before its shearers,
So He did not open His mouth.

(Prophecy fulfilled in Matthew 27:12-14, 1 Peter 2:23)[32]

⁸ By oppression and judgment He was taken away;
And as for His generation, who considered
That He was cut off out of the land of the living
For the transgression of my people, to whom the stroke was due?
⁹ His grave was assigned with wicked men,
Yet He was with a rich man in His death,
Because He had done no violence,
Nor was there any deceit in His mouth.
¹⁰ But the Lord was pleased
To crush Him, putting Him to grief;
If He would render Himself as a guilt offering,
He will see His offspring,

He will prolong His days,
And the good pleasure of the Lord will prosper in His hand.
[11] As a result of the anguish of His soul,
He will see it and be satisfied;
By His knowledge the Righteous One,
My Servant, will justify the many,
As He will bear their iniquities.
[12] Therefore, I will allot Him a portion with the great,
And He will divide the booty with the strong;
Because He poured out Himself to death,
And was numbered with the transgressors;
Yet He Himself bore the sin of many,
And interceded for the transgressors.

Now for Psalm 22. Notice that this psalm was immediately applied to King David, and ultimately to the Messiah, Jesus Christ.

Psalm 22:1–31

[22] My God, my God, why have You forsaken me?
Far from my deliverance are the words of
my groaning.

(Prophecy fulfilled in Matthew 27:46)

² O my God, I cry by day, but You do not answer;
And by night, but I have no rest.
³ Yet You are holy,
O You who are enthroned upon the praises of Israel.
⁴ In You our fathers trusted;
They trusted and You delivered them.
⁵ To You they cried out and were delivered;
In You they trusted and were not disappointed.
⁶ But I am a worm and not a man,
A reproach of men and despised by the people.
⁷ All who see me sneer at me;
They separate with the lip, they wag the head, saying,
⁸ "Commit yourself to the Lord; let Him deliver him;
Let Him rescue him, because He delights in him."

(Prophecy fulfilled in Luke 23:35-36)

⁹ Yet You are He who brought me forth from the womb;
You made me trust when upon my mother's breasts.
¹⁰ Upon You I was cast from birth;
You have been my God from my mother's womb.
¹¹ Be not far from me, for trouble is near;
For there is none to help.

^{12} Many bulls have surrounded me;
Strong bulls of Bashan have encircled me.
^{13} They open wide their mouth at me,
As a ravening and a roaring lion.
^{14} I am poured out like water,
And all my bones are out of joint;
My heart is like wax;
It is melted within me.
^{15} My strength is dried up like a potsherd,
And my tongue cleaves to my jaws;

(Prophecy fulfilled in John 19:28)

And You lay me in the dust of death.
^{16} For dogs have surrounded me;
A band of evildoers has encompassed me;
They pierced my hands and my feet.
^{17} I can count all my bones.
They look, they stare at me;
^{18} They divide my garments among them,
And for my clothing they cast lots.

(Prophecy fulfilled in Mark 15:24)[33]

^{19} But You, O Lord, be not far off;
O You my help, hasten to my assistance.
^{20} Deliver my soul from the sword,
My only life from the power of the dog.

²¹ Save me from the lion's mouth;
From the horns of the wild oxen You answer me.
²² I will tell of Your name to my brethren;
In the midst of the assembly I will praise You.
²³ You who fear the Lord, praise Him;
All you descendants of Jacob, glorify Him,
And stand in awe of Him, all you descendants of Israel.
²⁴ For He has not despised nor abhorred the affliction of the afflicted;
Nor has He hidden His face from him;
But when he cried to Him for help, He heard.
²⁵ From You comes my praise in the great assembly;
I shall pay my vows before those who fear Him.
²⁶ The afflicted will eat and be satisfied;
Those who seek Him will praise the Lord.
Let your heart live forever!
²⁷ All the ends of the earth will remember and turn to the Lord,
And all the families of the nations will worship before You.
²⁸ For the kingdom is the Lord's
And He rules over the nations.
²⁹ All the prosperous of the earth will eat and worship,
All those who go down to the dust will bow before Him,
Even he who cannot keep his soul alive.

> *[30] Posterity will serve Him;*
> *It will be told of the Lord*
> *to the coming generation.*
> *[31] They will come and will declare His*
> *righteousness*
> *To a people who will be born, that He has*
> *performed it.*

If you read Psalm 22 alongside the accounts of Jesus' crucifixion in the four gospels, it's hard to avoid concluding the gospel accounts and Psalm 22 are indeed describing the same events. And the fact that the details in the New Testament are somewhat different means the New Testament writers did not merely copy Old Testament writings and apply them to Jesus. We must also remember that crucifixion did not even exist when Psalm 22 was written.

These fulfilled prophecies give us good reason to believe the Bible is not only God's authoritative Word, it is reliable as truth and dependable for future prophecies.

CHAPTER 18

HAS THE BIBLE BEEN CORRUPTED OVER TIME?

Over the years the Bible has been translated into many languages, and there seems to be new versions of the Bible coming out every several years or so. But how can I trust that a Bible I buy today is accurately representing what was originally written?

Let's first learn what the difference between a translation and a version is. A translation of the Bible is simply changing what's written in one language into a different language. But there are also many different versions of the Bible in any given language. For example, there are many versions of the Bible that have been translated into the English language. Why all these English versions? It all comes down to variations of the English language. For example, a well-known version of the Bible, the King James Bible, uses an old English speaking style that is not popular today. Whereas newer English versions of the Bible are written in a more modern language variation. Some versions are written in a more "word for word" style, while others are written in a more "thought for thought" style. Most people don't read the Bible in its original language since it was originally written in Hebrew, Aramaic, and Greek.

Therefore, most of us read a version of the Bible that has been translated into our own language.[34]

To sum up, a translation of the Bible refers to whatever language the Bible is written in, while a version refers to the variation, or speaking style, of that specific language. But with all these translations and versions, aren't there errors due to all these copies and rewrites?

Have you ever played the telephone game? The game goes like this: Several people sit side by side and one person starts the game by whispering something into the ear of the person sitting next to him/her. Then that person whispers what they heard into the ear of the person sitting next to them, and this goes on from person to person until the very last person hears the whispered message. Then the last person says the message out loud, and invariably, the spoken message is far from the original whispered message. This is because each time the message was whispered, there is a chance for errors to be made in accurately repeating what was heard. The chance for error increases as more people play the game.

Well, most people think all these Bible translations and versions are written the same way the telephone game is played. I used to think this too. But that's not the case. Any new translation or version of the Bible that comes out today does not rely on the most recent Bibles that have been printed. Instead, the translators actually go back to the earliest copies of Scripture and write new translations or versions from these ancient manuscripts. This is why you can be sure you won't end up with errors like in the telephone game.

The original texts of biblical law were kept in the ark as described in the Old Testament, then later kept in the temple sanctuary in Jerusalem. Copies of these original texts could then be made and consulted by anyone who had questions. Throughout time, approximately around the second century BC, the writers (scribes) became a distinct political party made up of highly educated people affiliated with the Pharisees.

A "copyist" had the task of reproducing text as accurately as possible. We can identify occasions where mistakes were made based on variations between texts. The close similarity between different copies of the text, originating from different eras and received in different languages, is remarkable. In fact, the discovery of the Dead Sea Scrolls has highlighted the extraordinary accuracy of this process. Even though some copies don't always agree, due to misspellings, damage to a scroll that leaves illegible or missing words, omission or addition of a word, and so forth, no major item of Christian belief is compromised.

A modern-day example of this would be when we receive a phone text that is obviously misspelled or has missing words. For example, if you received a phone text that read, "I can't meet at Starbucks, running late. Can we meet for coofee tomorrow?" you immediately know the word "coofee" is misspelled but the message isn't compromised by this mistake.

The Bibles we read today are made by going all the way back to the earliest copies we have of ancient manuscripts. They are not made by playing the telephone game, and great care is taken when making the Bible you read today.

CHAPTER 19

THE DEAD SEA SCROLLS

We no longer have any original ancient manuscripts of Scripture, but we do have large numbers of copies. How, then, can we be sure these copies are accurate? This brings in the amazing discovery of the Dead Sea Scrolls.

What are the Dead Sea Scrolls? They are a collection of some forty thousand inscribed fragments, and from these fragments, five hundred books have been reconstructed. Most of these discovered ancient writings are copies of the Old Testament, dating from more than a century before the birth of Jesus. This discovery is so important because the oldest Hebrew manuscripts of the Old Testament we had before the Dead Sea Scrolls were discovered were dated from 900 AD.

The writings from the Dead Sea Scrolls were compared to copies we already had from 900 AD to see how accurate the copies were. And in particular, the book of Isaiah, which is an Old Testament book written by a prophet named Isaiah, was found to be "word for word identical with our standard Hebrew Bible in more than 95 percent of the text ... The 5 percent of variation consisted chiefly of obvious slips of the pen and variations in spelling," according to Gleason Archer, author of *A Survey of Old Testament Introduction*.[35]

How were the Dead Sea Scrolls discovered?

Ralph Earle gives the account:

"The story of this discovery is one of the most fascinating tales of modern times. In February or March of 1947, a Bedouin shepherd boy named Muhammad was searching for a lost goat. He tossed a stone into a hole in a cliff on the west side of the Dead Sea, about eight miles south of Jericho. To his surprise he heard the sound of shattering pottery. Investigating, he discovered an amazing sight. On the floor of the cave were several large jars containing leather scrolls, wrapped in linen cloth. Because the jars were carefully sealed, the scrolls had been preserved in excellent condition for nearly 1,900 years."[36]

Dr. W. F. Albright of Johns Hopkins University, who was widely recognized as the Dean of American Biblical Archaeologists, wrote, "My heartiest congratulations on the greatest manuscript discovery of modern times ... What an absolutely incredible find! And there can happily not be the slightest doubt in the world about the genuineness of the manuscript."[37] He dated the Isaiah scroll about 100 BC.

The Dead Sea Scrolls travel around the world for display at various museums. My husband and I saw them while on vacation in Alabama and it was absolutely fascinating. If you ever get a chance to see them, I highly recommend it. I found it quite amazing and interesting that the museum constantly records the humidity and temperature of the room the scrolls are displayed in and transmits this information to the authorities in Jerusalem so they can make sure the scrolls are being kept in perfect condition.

The Dead Sea Scrolls prove that the earliest copies we have of the Old Testament are extraordinarily accurate. And it is these copies of Scripture that translators go to when developing new translations and versions of the Bible. This is why you can have confidence in the accuracy of the Old Testament.

But what about New Testament accuracy?

CHAPTER 20

NEW TESTAMENT ACCURACY

It is extremely vital to have accurate manuscripts from which we get the New Testament. After all, the claims about Jesus, heaven, hell, and future judgment all hang in the balance. A lot is at stake. As with the Old Testament, we also do not have any original manuscripts of the New Testament. So the same question remains, "How reliable are the copies we have?"

Two criteria are used in determining the accuracy of the New Testament copies:

1. How much time elapsed from when the original document was written to when the copy was made?

Generally speaking, the closer in date a copy is made to when the original document was written, the more reliable the copy is since it is less likely to be corrupt. For example, when police are trying to get information about a crime, it's always better to question the witnesses right after the crime was committed instead of waiting weeks, months, or years. Why? Because their memories of what happened would be more reliable. The same logic applies to why it's always better to have less time elapse from when an original document was written to when any copies were made.

The following chart compares four well-known historical writings to the New Testament, showing how much time elapsed from when the writing was originally written to when the earliest copies were made.[38] We can see from the chart that very little time elapsed from when the New Testament was written to when copies of the entire New Testament were finished in 325 AD. This smaller gap in time makes these copies more reliable in their accuracy.

COMPARISON OF
HISTORICAL WRITINGS AND NEW TESTAMENT

Writer & Work	Date Written	Earliest Copies	Time Gap	# of Copies
Homer Iliad	800 B.C.	415 B.C.	385 years	1900+
Caesar Gallic Wars	100-44 B.C.	9th c. A.D.	944 years	251
Plato	400 B.C.	3rd c. B.C.	100 years	238
Aristotle	384-322 B.C.	1100 A.D.	1400 years	49
New Testament	50-100 A.D.	130-325 A.D.	80-225 years	23,986

Another thing to look for is:

2. How many copies do we have?

Let's use the example of hearing witnesses testify in a court case. What would be better, to have one witness testify or to have two witnesses testify? Of course the answer is two. The more witnesses we have, the more information we have to compare testimonies and therefore, have a clearer picture of what happened. The same goes for having more copies rather than fewer of the New Testament. If you have a large amount of copies in which they all say the same thing, then you will be more confident that they are accurate. If ninety-nine copies say one thing and one copy says something different, then you can be pretty sure that one copy is wrong.

Also, the more copies you have, the better you can reconstruct the original message. For example, if you had ten copies of your family's ancestry, it would be much easier to have a complete picture of your bloodline than if you had only one copy. That's because if there were any marks, rips, or holes in the one copy you had, you wouldn't have anything to look to in order to fill in the gaps. But if you had ten copies, you could easily look through them to see what information was missing from the one that had a rip in it.

The previous chart shows the New Testament has 23,986 copies, while Homer's *Iliad* has only 1,900 in comparison. I never hear anyone question the authenticity of these other ancient writings listed on the chart, yet we have far fewer copies of these writings in comparison to the New Testament. This is a major factor in favor of the Bible's accuracy.

Here's another chart to illustrate this point:

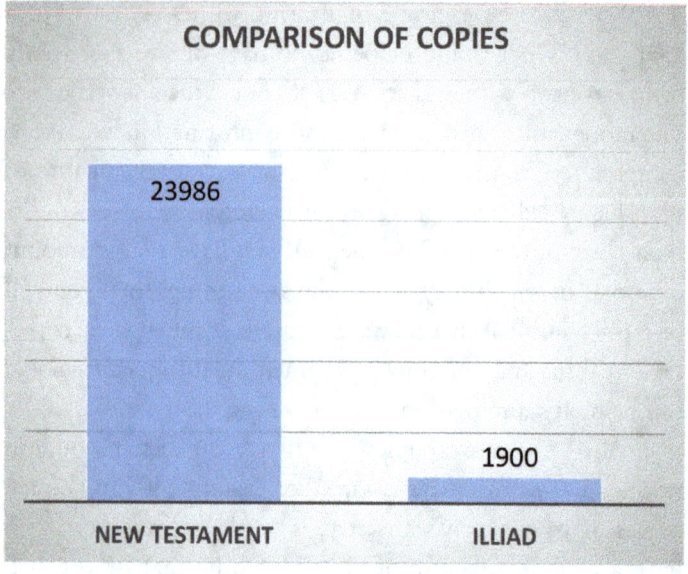

As you can see, the New Testament accuracy is extremely reliable since the copies were made so close to the originals in terms of years, and since we have an extraordinary amount of copies with which we can compare them. No other ancient manuscript passes the test like the New Testament manuscripts do.

CHAPTER 21

ARE THERE CONTRADICTIONS IN THE BIBLE?

This is a great question. Every time I have looked at what seems to be a contradiction in the Bible, it turns out that it isn't a contradiction at all, but rather it's due to our own misunderstanding of what's written. Each supposed contradiction usually falls into one of four categories:

1. Context

Any passage of Scripture has to be understood within the context in which it was written. I've seen many verses twisted and misunderstood due to simply taking them out of context. For example, one passage of the Bible says that God does not repent (change His mind), whereas another passage says God did repent. Don't these contradict each other? Well, let's look at the context:

> *"God is not a man, that He should lie,*
> *Nor a son of man, that He should repent;*
> *Has He said, and will He not do it?*
> *Or has He spoken, and will He not make it good?" (Numbers 23:19)*

While a different verse says:

So the Lord changed His mind about the harm which He said He would do to His people. (Exodus 32:14)

The context of the Numbers verse is describing the perfect character of God and His faithfulness in carrying out His will. Since God is perfect, He does not need to repent like we do.

The context of the Exodus verse is that the nation of Israel had sinned against God, so God was telling Moses that He was going to destroy them. But before this, God had already promised to deliver the nation of Israel from the bondage of slavery in Egypt and to bring them into the promised land. Exodus 32:14 takes place after God delivered the Israelites from Egypt but before He brought them into the promised land. So Moses stepped in and pleaded with God on behalf of the Israelites, pointing to the promise God previously made.

Now here's the point: the promises of God are irrevocable. They are divine, unchangeable decrees. God will not change His mind, or repent, from carrying out His divine decrees, which is exactly what Numbers 23:19 is describing.

But a divine decree is not the same as a divine intention. God intended to punish the nation of Israel for their sin, yet He did not carry out that intention due to Moses interceding on their behalf. God won't go back on His promises, but He can use various means in how He will carry out His promises. God used Moses' entreaty as a means to bring the nation of Israel into the promised land, which is exactly what God originally promised to do. This demonstrates the faithfulness of God to His Word, which is exactly what Numbers 23:19 says. There is no contradiction when you understand the context of these verses.

2. Hyperbole

Some supposed contradictions fall into this category when Scripture uses hyperbole to make a point. For example, one of God's commandments is to honor your father and mother (Exodus 20:12). But then Jesus says this in Luke's gospel:

"If anyone comes to Me, and does not hate his own father and mother and wife and children and brothers and sisters, yes, and even his own life, he cannot be My disciple." (Luke 14:26)

Wait a minute, is God promoting hate? I thought God commanded us to love one another, so why does He say we must hate our own families in order to follow Him? Isn't this a contradiction? The answer is that Jesus is using hyperbole to make a point. And the point is this: Jesus says that if you want to be His disciple, then He requires full devotion. Jesus was calling His disciples to cultivate such a devotion to Him that their attachment to anything or anyone else, including their own lives, would seem like hatred in comparison.

When reading the Bible, it's also critical to read all the verses that talk about any one topic. When we do this we get a better understanding of what's being taught. We can look to another verse on this same topic and by doing so, we get a fuller understanding. In Matthew 10:37 Jesus says:

> *"He who loves father or mother more than Me is not worthy of Me; and he who loves son or daughter more than Me is not worthy of Me."*

In this verse, Jesus doesn't even use the word *hate*. Instead He simply states that our love for others should not supersede the love we have for Him. We are commanded to love others but not over and above the love and devotion we have for God. What if your parents told you to cheat, steal, or kill? Are you supposed to do what they say out of "honoring" them? Of course not. We are to love and honor our parents, but not if it means disobeying God. Jesus calls for full devotion to Himself above any other relationship, and He uses the most common relationships we have, family, to make His point.

3. Different calendars and time measures

Some perceived contradictions in Scripture are due to this third reason, the use of different calendars and time measuring. Sometimes the dates recorded in Scripture when describing the same event are different. This seems like a problem, but it's not when one passage is using one calendar while another passage is using a different calendar. The same goes with time.

The Gospels describe the crucifixion of Christ, and in doing so, the time of Jesus' crucifixion is recorded. So why are these times different?

Mark 15:25 says,

"It was the third hour when they crucified Him."

While John 19:14 says,

"Now it was the day of preparation for the Passover; it was about the sixth hour. And he said to the Jews, 'Behold, your King!'"

These verses seem to contradict each other, but when you understand that the Jews and Romans had different ways of reckoning time, then there is no contradiction. Mark seems to be using the Jewish method of reckoning time in his gospel, while in John's gospel, he seems to be using the Roman method.

Added to this, there was a difference among the Jews in the way they reckoned the beginning and ending of days. Jews in the north calculated days from sunrise to sunrise, while Jews in the southern part reckoned days from sunset to sunset. This difference also answers the supposed contradiction of whether or not Jesus was crucified on Passover Day.

On the basis of these differences in time reckoning, the seeming contradictions in the Gospels are easily explained.

4. Eyewitness accounts

When eyewitnesses are questioned in a courtroom setting, it's common for each witness to give varying information describing the same scene. For instance, if several witnesses all saw the same person running from a bank robbery, they usually pick up on different details in describing that person. One witness may notice if the person was wearing a hat, whereas another witness may not notice the hat but rather notice what shoes he/she was wearing. But just because they all notice different aspects doesn't mean they didn't see the same person.

In fact, if all the witnesses gave the same exact account, their stories would seem made up, or rehearsed. So when eyewitnesses give varying information, it actually lends credibility to their stories since each person picks up on different things. This is why it's good to have more than one witness, so we can have a more complete understanding of what happened.

The same is true in the eyewitness accounts given in the gospels of Matthew and John. Both gospels give an account of Jesus' resurrection, yet Matthew records one angel at the tomb, while John records two angels. Why the difference? The answer is simple. Just because one account records one angel does not mean there was only one angel at the scene. Here are the verses so you can see for yourself:

> ***And behold, a severe earthquake had occurred, for an angel of the Lord descended from heaven and came and rolled away the stone and sat upon it. And his appearance was like lightning, and his clothing as white as snow. (Matthew 28:2–3)***

But Mary was standing outside the tomb weeping; and so, as she wept, she stooped and looked into the tomb; and she saw two angels in white sitting, one at the head and one at the feet, where the body of Jesus had been lying.
(John 20:11-12)

Matthew's account is describing what one angel did, while John's account describes what Mary saw when she looked inside the tomb. These are describing different moments during the same scene. Just because one angel rolled away the stone doesn't mean there was only one angel there. In fact, these two accounts give us a broader viewpoint as to what occurred at the scene. So when reading Scripture, we not only have to understand the context with which any one passage was written, we also have to read all the passages that pertain to the same topic to have a more complete picture.

I believe the most important verse in the whole Bible is Psalm 119:160a, which says,

"The sum of Your word is truth."

I think this is the most important verse because so many of us can too easily take one verse and develop an incomplete understanding of what's written. For us to know the full truth of any topic of Scripture, we must study each and every verse that addresses that same topic. Presenting a "half-truth" as if it's the "whole truth" is misleading. Truth is the sum of all Scripture.

TRUTH EXISTS

CHAPTER 22

THE DIVERSITY OF THE BIBLE IS EVIDENCE IT IS GOD'S WORD

The Bible is a collection of sixty-six smaller books that are divided into two parts: the Old Testament and the New Testament. These sixty-six books were written by various writers over a period of approximately 1,500 years. They were written on three different continents—Asia, Africa, and Europe—and were originally written in three different languages—Hebrew, Aramaic, and Greek.

The Old Testament contains thirty-nine of the sixty-six books and chronicles God's relationship with mankind from creation up to approximately four hundred years before Jesus Christ was born. The first eleven chapters of the Bible describe God's interaction with mankind as a whole. Then in Genesis chapter 12, God begins to focus on the Jewish nation, which begins with a man named Abraham. God's focus is on the Jewish nation throughout the remainder of the Old Testament as He is setting the stage for the birth of the promised Messiah, who comes from the Jewish nation. The first mention of this promise is in Genesis 3:15.

The Old Testament is also the Jewish Bible.

The New Testament contains twenty-seven of the sixty-six books and covers a period of about one hundred years beginning with the birth of Jesus, the promised Messiah. The life, death, and resurrection of Jesus are chronicled in the first four books of the New Testament, which are referred to as the four Gospels, which are then followed by letters to the church. The very last book of the Bible, Revelation, returns to God's focus toward mankind as a whole, as the world is prepared for final judgment at Jesus' Second Coming.

The Old and the New Testament combined is the Christian Bible.

These sixty-six books that make up the Christian Bible have many different writing styles, moods, and topics. They were written during various climates, such as prosperity, despair, war, and peace. Yet with the wide variety of writers, and with the span of 1,500 years over which these books were written, they still amazingly flow with one another in the overall story and message of God's plan to offer salvation through Jesus Christ. This continuity throughout the Bible is due to God, through the guidance and inspiration of the Holy Spirit, moving through each writer to accurately pen exactly what God wanted to convey, without obscuring each writer's own individuality, personality, and writing style.

The message of the Old Testament and New Testament goes hand in hand as the Old Testament sets the stage for the New Testament. How? By teaching human beings have not lived up to the purpose for which they were created, which is to obey God in order to reflect His holy image, demonstrated though holy living. Each human has instead chosen to follow his/her own desires and will, rather than God's, by disobeying His commandments. This is called sin.

The Bible not only reveals sinfulness but also teaches God must judge sin since He is holy and just. The Old Testament foretells the future coming of a Messiah, a Savior, sent to save humans from being judged by God according to their sins. The New Testament reveals that this Messiah, this Savior, is Jesus.

The Bible teaches that there are three separate, distinct Persons in God: God the Father, God the Son, and God the Holy Spirit. Jesus, who is sometimes referred to as the Second Person of the Trinity, is God Himself, and came to live as a man in order to fulfill God's commands by living in perfect obedience. The sinless life Jesus lived qualifies Him to offer Himself as the perfect sacrifice to atone for sin.

(The definition of *atone* is to make amends; to provide or serve as reparation or compensation for something bad or unwelcome.)[39]

But why? Why did Jesus have to die?

In the Old Testament, God told the Israelites that blood was necessary to atone for their sins. We can read God explaining this in Leviticus 17:11:

"For the life of the flesh is in the blood, and I have given it to you on the altar to make atonement for your souls; for it is the blood by reason of the life that makes atonement."

Therefore, the Old Testament was filled with ongoing animal sacrifices that the Jewish people offered to God because they sinned against Him. But shedding the blood of animals could not take away sins committed by people. Only the blood of a human can atone for sins committed by a human.

We read about this in Hebrews 10:4:

> ***For it is impossible for the blood of bulls and goats to take away sins.***

So why all the animal sacrifices? Because God was teaching the Israelites, and us, how serious He is about sin. Plus, all the repeated animal sacrifices throughout the Old Testament were pointing to a future sacrifice that the Messiah would offer. This is why Jesus is also referred to as "the Lamb of God." The blood of Jesus was able to atone for sins committed by humans since His blood was that of a holy, sinless, perfectly obedient man. Jesus' sacrifice of Himself, therefore, put an end to the repeated animal sacrifices, replacing the Old Testament with the New Testament, just as Hebrews 10:9b says:

> ***He takes away the first in order to establish the second.***

The Bible also teaches that God raised Jesus from the dead, proving Jesus' sacrificial death on the cross was sufficient to atone for sin. God now offers forgiveness to anyone who believes in Jesus, following Him out of grateful love for what He did to provide atonement. This love for Jesus is demonstrated through obedience to Him.

The overall message of the Bible from beginning to end is so consistent that this in and of itself is strong evidence in favor of the Bible's authority as being God's Word. What other book that contains sixty-six smaller books, written by so many different writers over such a long period of time, has such consistency? In fact, the consistency of the Bible is staggering in light of the vast diversity in which it was written.

TRUTH EXISTS

CHAPTER 23

WHY FORGIVENESS IS AN EXPRESSION OF LOVE

Forgiveness goes way beyond one person just saying to another, "You're forgiven." You see, the person who's doing the forgiving has to also incur a debt in the form of some sort of loss. For example, let's say I stole money from you and spent it all. Then you find out about it and have chosen to forgive me. By forgiving me, you not only wipe my slate clean, but you also incur a debt since I can't pay back the money that I stole from you.

Or let's say I spread gossip about you all over town. When you hear about it, you choose to forgive me. But even though you choose to forgive me, you still incur a loss because you experienced hurt and disappointment by being slandered. I hurt you by what I did and I can't do anything to put things back to the way they were before I gossiped about you. The damage has already been done.

Let's take it a step further and say I committed murder. Let's also say the family of the person I murdered has chosen to forgive me. I can't make it up to them by giving them back their loved one, can I? So the family has not only incurred a loss by losing their loved one, but they also chose to forgive me, knowing full well I can never pay them back.

Do you see what a huge gift forgiveness is? Do you see why we have such a hard time forgiving others? We like to have things even; if you take from me, then I want to naturally take the same from you. But that's not how God has chosen to interact with us. The Bible teaches that God offers us forgiveness for our sins, knowing full well we can never pay Him back.

It's important to understand what forgiveness is as well as what it isn't. Forgiving someone does not mean what they did is okay. Forgiving someone does not mean you forget either. But even though you can't forget what they did, it doesn't mean you should "remember" what they did by bringing up the offense over and over, or by holding on to a grudge. In fact, forgiving someone means you no longer hold that offense against them. Forgiveness is offered because you would rather be reconciled to the person who hurt you instead of allowing the offense to keep you separated.

Our sinful choices have consequences that can't be erased. The damage has already been done, and the damage is that our sin separates us from God and this separation lasts for all eternity. This damage that sin causes can't be undone by doing good deeds either, just as the damage in the above examples can't be undone. Forgiveness is not only a gift, it's the only thing that can heal broken relationships.

TRUTH EXISTS

CHAPTER 24

GOOD NEWS

Why would God choose to treat us so graciously by sending His Son to die in our place so that we can be forgiven?

The Bible says why in John 3:16:

"For God so loved the world, that He gave His only begotten Son, that whoever believes in Him shall not perish, but have eternal life."

God did this out of love for the very people He created. This message is called the gospel, which means "good news." But before we can truly appreciate the good news, we have to understand the bad news.

The Bible teaches not only do our sins separate us from God, but there is nothing we can do to make up for our sins. You see, our sins actually earn wages and these wages are described as death. But this isn't just a physical death. Since God is an eternal God, then our sins have earned and deserve eternal death. Sin, therefore, has eternal consequences.

For the wages of sin is death, but the free gift of God is eternal life in Christ Jesus our Lord. (Romans 6:23)

Notice the word "wages" in this verse. We all know that when we do a job or go to work for a living, we receive a paycheck. The paycheck we receive is the wages we've earned and deserve. Well, in a similar way, this verse teaches that the wages we earn and deserve for the sins we commit is eternal death, which is another way of saying our sins have earned and deserve hell.

But notice the words "free gift" in that same verse. God offers us the opposite of what we deserve, which means eternal life is a free gift. So even though we, as sinners, deserve eternal death (hell), God offers us what we don't deserve: eternal life (heaven). This is indeed good news!

God is not only a God who loves, He is also holy and just. This means He must judge sin. For example, in our judicial system, criminals are judged for the crimes they commit. We even become outraged when we see a judge go easy on criminals because we expect justice, especially when we are the victim. Well, since God is perfectly holy and just, He must judge sin and we would be outraged if He didn't, especially when we are the victim of sin. In fact, after various types of horrific events that occur throughout the world, we sometimes hear people say things like, "Where is God?" This is because we want God to do something. We want justice.

But herein lies the problem: if we want God to judge sin, then that means each of us will be found guilty since we all have sinned. We can't tell God what to judge and what not to judge. This is why the cross is so meaningful to Christians: it symbolizes the place where God demonstrated both His justice and His love. God demonstrated justice by judging sin, while also demonstrating love because Jesus was the one being judged in our place. As we learned in the previous chapter, forgiveness is always costly since the one who forgives incurs a debt of some sort. Forgiving us was extremely costly for God since it cost Him the very life of His Son, Jesus.

The Bible also teaches Jesus rose from the dead and He gives eternal life to anyone who believes in Him. So on one hand, the gospel is exclusive since the only way to receive eternal life is through faith in Jesus. But on the other hand, it's inclusive since this offer is for anyone who believes. Therefore, when people end up in hell, it's not because God is rejecting them, it's because they have rejected God's offer of forgiveness through the gospel.

Jesus clearly states there are only two options when faced with the gospel:

> *"He who believes in Him is not judged; he who does not believe has been judged already, because he has not believed in the name of the only begotten Son of God." (John 3:18)*

Did you catch that? If you believe, you won't be judged. If you don't believe, you are judged. Either we believe Jesus provided atonement for our sins when He was crucified or if we don't believe, then we will be judged according to the wages our sins have earned. Since belief or unbelief are the only options, it's clear there is no other way to get to heaven. In fact, to say we can get to heaven without faith in Jesus would be making God a cruel God. What kind of God would send His Son to shed His own blood through a horrible death if none of that was necessary for us to get to heaven?

In chapter 22 we learned that the shedding of blood is necessary to provide atonement for sin (Leviticus 17:11). The Bible is also clear that without the shedding of blood there is no forgiveness.

> *And according to the Law, one may almost say, all things are cleansed with blood, and without shedding of blood there is no forgiveness. (Hebrews 9:22)*

God wants us to know we have to enter heaven on His terms. For example, if you went to a baseball game and gave them a soccer ticket, do you really think you'll get into the game? Of course not. You have to enter the game on their terms, not yours. It's the same with heaven. Heaven is God's home, and we have to enter on His terms. We won't be able to stand before God hoping all the good things we've done outweigh all the bad things we've done, or by trying to be a good person. Those aren't His terms.

TRUTH EXISTS

CHAPTER 25

IF GOD IS LOVING, THEN WHY DOES HE ALLOW SO MUCH SUFFERING IN THE WORLD?

This is by far the most common objection to the Bible. And understandably so. I've asked this question myself. The answer is this: the reason why there is suffering in the world is *because* God is loving. In order for love to be genuine, it cannot be forced or coerced, which means there has to be the option to not love. Can you imagine how empty and meaningless our relationships would be if all the people in your life were "programmed" to love you and had no choice in the matter?

God did not make human puppets. He made us in His image, and since God is a God who loves, He also made us with the capacity to love. This means He blessed us with the freedom to choose. We can use that freedom to either love Him or not. Suffering, therefore, is the consequence of choosing to not love God and others the way we should. The eternal consequence of sin is eternal death as we learned in chapter 24, but the temporal consequence of sin is suffering in the world.

Here's a picture of a popular toy dog robot. It's a fun toy and can do a lot of tricks.

But a toy will never come close to this:

A puppy is so much better than a toy because you can actually experience genuine love for, and from, a real dog. The robot may be programmed to wag its tail when it sees you, but since you know it's not genuine, it's not real love, and therefore meaningless.

The same goes for us. God wants us to love Him and others from a heart of sincerity, which is why He gave us the freedom to choose to love or not. We sin when we choose to not love the way God commands us to. This is why God equates loving Him with obeying Him since obedience is a choice.

Jesus says in John 14:15,

"If you love Me, you will keep My commandments."

This world would be a completely different place if everyone obeyed God. Why? Because God's commandments show us what love looks like. As you read the Ten Commandments below, notice how the first four are examples of what it looks like to love God, while the remaining six are examples of what it looks like to love others.

Here they are:

Exodus 20:3-17
1. *You shall have no other gods before Me.*
2. *You shall not make for yourself an idol or worship or serve them.*
3. *You shall not take the name of the Lord your God in vain.*

4. *Remember the Sabbath day, to keep it holy.*
5. *Honor your father and mother.*
6. *You shall not murder.*
7. *You shall not commit adultery.*
8. *You shall not steal.*
9. *You shall not bear false witness against your neighbor.*
10. *You shall not covet anything belonging to your neighbor.*

If you love God, then you simply won't have any other gods instead of Him or take His name in vain. And if you love others, then you won't lie to them or steal from them. In fact, Romans 13:10 says,

> *"Love does no wrong to a neighbor; therefore love is the fulfillment of the law."*

The suffering we see in the world today is the direct result of the first man and woman, Adam and Eve, choosing to sin by disobeying God. The Bible teaches Adam and Eve did not disobey God for themselves alone but for the entire human race. Adam, who represented the human race, went on to produce a human race marked by sin. Our sinful choices not only prove we each have inherited a sinful nature from Adam but are a transgression of God's laws. Sin, therefore, not only offends and hurts others since it is lovelessness, but it is ultimately rebellion toward God.

The Bible teaches the sinful nature we have inherited from Adam involves a condition in which our hearts are corrupted and inclined toward evil. We sin when we choose disobedience because it seems more attractive or reasonable. We are commanded by God to use the freedom of choice to love Him and others, yet we are easily drawn to prefer the opposite.[40]

God has given humans immense power because our choices have consequences. We can easily be the innocent victim of someone else's sin. For example, you can be walking down the street and a random bullet kills you, or a drunk driver slams into a store, injuring dozens. So why doesn't God do something to prevent these consequences?

I'll list three reasons.

1. Because the world is also filled with beautiful expressions of love, compassion, kindness, and joy. If God made a world in which there were no consequences for our choices, therefore eliminating suffering, then that would also eliminate all the wonderful consequences of expressing love. And what meaning would life have if there were no consequences for our choices? What would be the point of choosing good over evil? The fact that our choices matter, due to the consequences they bring, gives life meaning.

2. Someone might ask, "Well, why doesn't God just eliminate all the bad choices we make and keep the good?" Well, if He did that, then none of us would be here since we all are guilty of making bad choices. It's either eliminate the source of bad choices (people) or make human puppets who are incapable of making bad choices, which brings us back to the original point of no longer having genuine love.

   Let's say God eliminated the top 10 percent of all the evil in the world. Maybe that would include what we consider the worst offenders, like murderers and terrorists. Then we might want Him to eliminate the next 10 percent, like rapists and pedophiles. Why stop there? We would want the next 10 percent eliminated, like robbers, abusers, and cheats.

You see, even though you may not have murdered someone, if we keep adding offenses to the list of what we want eliminated, at some point, we all will be eliminated since we all have done something wrong.

Plus, if we're honest, we simply don't know how much evil and suffering God may be holding back already. What if all the suffering we see is a small percentage of what is actually possible? How many times have you had "close calls" in which you came close to getting hurt, but weren't?

3. The Bible teaches that God uses suffering for good purposes. For example, we would never know what comfort or compassion looks like if there were no suffering. After a major catastrophe, we see comfort and compassion demonstrated as people reach out to help those in need. We would also never know what forgiveness is if there was never anything to forgive. Since God is a God who comforts, forgives, and has mercy and compassion, He uses suffering to express these character traits to us. In addition to that, since we were made in His image, we can also choose to respond to suffering in the same way. Therefore, suffering

not only exposes character but can also build character.

We can most fully see the character of God through Jesus in how He responded to unspeakable suffering. He responded with grace, love, and truth, always reaching out, even to those who hurt Him the most. God demonstrates the depth of His love as He loves those who hurt Him. After all, love means the most when we deserve it the least.

So this is why a loving God allows suffering. Suffering is the consequence when humans use their God-given ability to choose sin over love. Suffering entered the world when our first parents, Adam and Eve, sinned. And each one of us adds to that suffering when we also choose sin over love.

CHAPTER 26

IS MORALITY EVIDENCE FOR GOD?

Where did we get the ability to tell right from wrong? Evolution has no explanation for this, but creationism does. Please don't overlook this fact. It's a big problem that evolution has no way of explaining human morality. This is important because this is what separates us from the rest of creation. We don't see animals living by moral standards because only humans have this unique attribute.

The Bible teaches that since God made humans in His own image, He gave us the ability to distinguish right from wrong. We see evidence of this as we witness our children exhibit this knowledge at a very young age. For example, if we tell our child to not touch a hot stove, inevitably the child will wait until we look away so they can reach out and touch it. They attempt this while we're not looking because they intuitively know that what they are about to do is wrong.

In fact, none of us ever had to learn how to lie. None of us ever had to take a class to learn how to lust. And none of us had to read a book to learn how to be jealous or wish harm to our enemies. To sum up, none of us ever had to learn how to sin. Not only do we naturally know how to sin, but we sometimes even hesitate before we are about to do something wrong because we wrestle in our souls as we contemplate it. Each of us has embedded within us a moral code, and we immediately know when we violate that code.

So where did this knowledge come from?

The Bible teaches that it comes from God. God gave us a conscience, and our conscience is the part of us that signals what we are about to do is wrong. It's also the part of us that causes guilt after we've done something wrong. We all know the difference between a guilty conscience and a clear conscience (Romans 2:14-15).

So if our conscience enables us to differentiate between right and wrong, then why don't we always follow our conscience? Why don't we always live up to that moral code each one of us has inside our souls? We violate our conscience because we like to take matters into our own hands just like the child did when touching the hot stove. None of us likes to be told what to do, so we prefer to be "judge" and decide for ourselves how to live. However, the problem with this is none of us can be an impartial judge when making decisions. This is because something else comes into play when we make choices—namely, desire. Desire plays a significant role in making moral decisions. Our conscience may tell us one thing, while our desires may tell us the opposite. Instead of making decisions that are purely based on right versus wrong, we are easily tempted to make decisions that favor our desires.

But is there an absolute moral standard? The Bible says yes. And that moral standard is set by God. This is why He gave us commandments: they teach us what is right and wrong. I wrote in chapter 1 that truth is true regardless of whether I know it, whether I agree with it, whether I like it or believe it. Therefore, regardless of how I feel about it, the Bible teaches that God is both Lawgiver and Judge.

But again, we don't like this very much. We like to run our lives according to how we see fit. But here's an example of how that scenario plays out:

John says, "I decide what's right and wrong in my own life. I'm the god of my universe."

Then Bill says in response, "Well, John, I'm going to kill you."

John says to Bill, "You can't kill me. You can't do that!"

Bill answers, "I'm the god of my universe and I say I can."

Do you see the problem with each of us wanting to decide for ourselves what is right and wrong? In fact, listen to what the world says and before long you will hear statements like, "Do whatever makes you happy, as long as it doesn't hurt anyone else." This may sound fine on the surface, but who are we to decide what may or may not hurt someone else? Throughout the ages, there have been many choices made in the pursuit of happiness that have indeed hurt others.

We are naturally drawn to any subjective morality code that allows us to live out our desires. This is why there are such deep differences when discussing issues like abortion, capital punishment, sex outside of marriage, and homosexuality. This is why there are so many differences in how families are run, or how countries are led.

The Bible teaches that God has given us a conscience to speak to our souls in the matter of what is right and wrong and we immediately know when we have made choices that go against our conscience. How could this have come from evolution? There's no good explanation for the existence of morality other than what the Bible says.

CHAPTER 27

CLOSING ARGUMENTS

The information we've looked at has been a lot, but certainly not exhaustive. As a juror, weigh the evidence. What evidence is there to support evolution? What evidence is there to support creationism? Evolution is a theory, so does the evidence support the theory? Creationism is based on the Bible, so does the Bible pass the test for its reliability? I wrote earlier that it amazes me how two people can look at the same evidence and come up with opposite conclusions. Here is a quote from a college textbook that I would like you to keep in mind while weighing the evidence for yourself:

"It's important to differentiate between the scientific data collected and the opinions scientists have about what the data mean. Scientists form and state opinions that may not always be supported by fact, just as other people do. Equally reputable scientists commonly state opinions that are in direct opposition."[41]

I agree with this textbook's statement. Scientists are humans too, which means they can come to conclusions that are not always supported by facts. A sincere pursuit of truth means you follow the evidence wherever it leads, not to where you want it to lead.

So let's sum up. Here are the claims of both naturalism and creationism:

Naturalism bases its faith on the Big Bang Theory, which suggests nearly 14 billion years ago all matter in the universe was concentrated into a very hot, tiny, dense region. Then for some unknown reason, this region expanded. Then about 4.5 billion years ago, the Earth cooled down and was a ball of rock. Then years of torrential rain fell upon the Earth, creating oceans. And swirling in the oceans was a babbling broth of complex chemicals, the chemicals of life. This chemical soup somehow came alive, evolving into all the forms of life throughout history.

Creationism puts faith in what the Bible reveals, which states that everything was created through specific divine acts of God as recorded in Genesis.

So, according to evolution, you and I came from rocks and rain, while creationism says we were created by God, who made humans in His own image.

A professor of philosophy at New York University, Thomas Nagel, admits why he is an atheist. He says he simply does not want there to be a God. He even admits that Darwinian evolution cannot provide adequate answers to why humans are capable of things that evolution simply cannot explain.[42] He also wrote a book titled *Mind and Cosmos: Why the Materialistic Neo-Darwinian Conception of Nature Is Almost Certainly False*. I respect Thomas Nagel's honesty as to why he's an atheist, but atheists such as Thomas Nagel have to ask themselves why they are willing to turn a blind eye to not only the possibility of God but evidence that points to God.[43]

I'm going to close with three quotes. The first quote is from a famous and outspoken atheist, Richard Dawkins:

"Faith is the very opposite of science. Faith is the belief in something without evidence. Science insists all the time on evidence—logical reasoning from evidence. Faith and science are completely incompatible."[44]

I would like to concentrate specifically on Dawkins's words "Faith is the belief in something without evidence." That statement couldn't be farther from the truth. Faith is the belief in something *because* of the evidence! As I stated previously, whatever you believe, it has to be by faith since none of us were there at the beginning of all that exists. So Dawkins's belief in evolution is indeed "by faith." Being an atheist means that Dawkins has faith God doesn't exist. Is his belief rooted in a subjective opinion or objective fact? If it's objective fact, then where's the evidence?

The second quote I would like to share is from Lee Strobel. Lee used to be an atheist but is now Christian. Here is a quote from him:

"To continue in atheism, I would need to believe that nothing produces everything, non-life produces life, randomness produces fine-tuning, chaos produces information, unconsciousness produces consciousness, and non-reason produces reason. I simply didn't have that much faith."[45]

And now, for the last quote. Erwin Lutzer, a well-known evangelical Christian pastor, author, and Bible teacher, once said during a teaching I heard on Moody Radio:

"If you want to believe the Bible is true, there is more than enough evidence. But if you don't want to believe the Bible is true, there will never be enough evidence."

I love this quote because it's very eye-opening as to why we believe certain things. I've heard people say that we can never know the truth about things like God or the beginning of the universe. Or others will say we're just not able to understand these things; they are way beyond our intellect, et cetera. But what if God really does exist and He gave us the truth and we have those answers in the Bible? If we don't believe the claims of the Bible, it's not due to a lack of evidence or not enough intellect. Instead, it all comes down to this: you will choose to believe what you want to believe.

Are your beliefs rooted in a sincere search for truth or are they rooted in your own wants and desires? Even if you do believe God exists, are you believing in God as He has revealed

Himself through the Bible or are you believing in a god you've made up in your own mind?

Truth is objective. Truth is universal. Truth is consistent. Truth exists.

> *For since the creation of the world His invisible attributes, His eternal power and divine nature, have been clearly seen, being understood through what has been made, so that they are without excuse. (Romans 1:20)*

ENDNOTES

1. *Merriam-Webster*, s.v. "truth."
2. *Merriam-Webster*, s.v.v. "naturalism," "macroevolution," "microevolution," "creationism."
3. "Charles Darwin Quotes II," Notable Quotes, http://notable-quotes.com/d/darwin_charles_ii.html.
4. "The Cambrian Explosion," All about Science, https://www.allaboutscience.org/the-cambrian-explosion.htm.
5. John C. Lennox, *God's Undertaker: Has Science Buried God?* (Oxford: Lion Books, 2007), 108, books.google.com.
6. Rory Galloway, "Galapagos Finches Caught in Act of Becoming New Species," *BBC News,* November 23, 2017, http://www.bbc.com/news/science-environment-42103058.
7. Ibid.
8. Quoted on Goodreads, https://www.goodreads.com/quotes/344545-if-it-could-be-demonstrated-that-any-complex-organ-existed.
9. "Irreducible Complexity: The Challenge to the Darwinian Evolutionary Explanations of Many Biochemical Structures," IDEA Center, http://www.ideacenter.org/contentmgr/showdetails.php/id/840.
10. "Human Evolution," *Heath Biology* (Lexington, MA: D. C. Heath and Company, 1991), 264, quoted in Richard Schaefer, *Creation: Behold: Worldviews and a New Scientific Awakening,* 109, books.google.com.
11. *Holt Earth Science* (1994), 282, quoted in "Creation and Evolution: Two Very Different Worldviews," Truth in Genesis, January 2, 2013, http://www.truthingenesis.com/2013/01/02/creation-and-evolution-two-very-different-worldviews/.
12. Paul Davies, "Was Life on Earth Born Lucky?" *New Scientist* 179, no. 2403 (July 12, 2003): 32, https://www.newscientist.com/article/mg17924034-700-was-life-on-earth-born-lucky/.

13 *The 1998 Grolier Multimedia Encyclopedia* (Danbury, CT: Grolier Interactive, Inc., 1998), fossil section.

14 Interview with Stephen Meyer, "Can DNA Prove the Existence of an Intelligent Designer?" *Biola Magazine*, Summer 2010, http://magazine.biola.edu/article/10-summer/can-dna-prove-the-existence-of-an-intelligent-desi/.

15 *Nature* 429 (May 27, 2004): 382–88.

16 Barney T. Maddox, MD, "Human Genome Project: Quantitative Disproof of Evolution," CEM facts sheet, cited in *Doubts about Evolution?* quoted in Jordan P. Niednagel, "Monkey Business," True Authority, http://trueauthority.com/cvse/monkeybusiness.htm.

17 Records from the University of Jeno trial in 1875, quoted in Richard Schaefer, *Creation: Behold: Worldviews and a New Scientific Awakening*, 56.

18 AZ Quotes, https://www.azquotes.com/quote/672737.

19 NOAA, "What Is a Hydrothermal Vent?" National Ocean Service website, last updated June 25, 2018, oceanservice.noaa.gov/facts/vents.html.

20 William D. Edwards, MD; Wesley J. Gabel, MDiv; Floyd E. Hosmer, MS, AMI, "On the Physical Death of Jesus Christ," JAMA 255, no. 11 (March 21, 1986): 1455–63, https://doi.org/10.1001/jama.1986.03370110077025.

21 Corey S. Powell, "The Universe May Be a Billion Years Younger Than We Thought. Scientists Are Scrambling to Figure Out Why," MACH, May 18, 2019, https://www.nbcnews.com/mach/science/universe-may-be-billion-years-younger-we-thought-scientists-are-ncna1005541.

22 Associated Press, "New Study Says Universe Expanding Faster and Is Younger," *Deseret News*, April 27, 2019, https://www.deseretnews.com/article/900067951/new-study-says-universe-expanding-faster-and-is-younger.html.

23 Dan Satherley, "The Star That's 'Older Than the Universe,'" *Newshub*, May 8, 2019, https://www.newshub.co.nz/home/world/2019/08/the-star-that-s-older-than-the-universe.html.

24 Ibid.

25 Jonathan Sarfati, "The Earth's Magnetic Field: Evidence That the Earth Is Young," Creation.com, March 1998, updated August 29, 2014, https://creation.com/the-earths-magnetic-field-evidence-that-the-earth-is-young.

26 D. Russell Humphreys, PhD, "Evidence for a Young World," *ICR*, June 1, 2005, https://www.icr.org/article/evidence-for-young-world.

27 J. E. O'Rourke, "Pragmatism versus Materialism in Stratigraphy," *American Journal of Science* 276 (January 1976): 51, quoted in "Circular Reasoning," *Practical Science* (blog), January 19, 2013, http://practicalscience7.blogspot.com/2013/01/circular-reasoning.html.

28 *Encyclopaedia Britannica*, 14th ed., s.v. "Geology," quoted in "Circular Reasoning," *Practical Science*.

29 Niles Eldredge, *Time Frames: The Rethinking of Darwinian Evolution and the Theory of Punctuated Equilibria* (New York: Simon and Schuster, 1985), 52, quoted in "Circular Reasoning," *Practical Science*.

30 Steven A. Austin, "Rapid Erosion at Mount St. Helens," *ICR*, 1984, https://www.icr.org/research/index/researchp_sa_r04/.

31 J. Warner Wallace, "Is There Any Evidence for Jesus Outside the Bible?" *Cold-Case Christianity* (blog), October 30, 2017, https://coldcasechristianity.com/writings/is-there-any-evidence-for-jesus-outside-the-bible/.

32 "Is the Isaiah 53 Prophecy Fulfilled by Jesus?" Belief Map, http://beliefmap.org/prophecy-fulfilled/jesus-isaiah-53.

33 Luke Wayne, "Is Psalm 22 a Messianic Prophecy?" CARM, April 3, 2017, https://carm.org/is-psalm-22-a-messianic-prophecy.

34 David and Pat Alexander, *Zondervan Handbook to the Bible* (Grand Rapids: Zondervan, 1999), 74.

35 Gleason Archer, *A Survey of Old Testament Introduction*, 28–29, quoted in Vince Latorre, "Was the Bible Tampered With? Not According to the Dead Sea Scrolls!" *The Bible Can Be Proven* (blog), http://thebiblecanbeproven.com/the-dead-sea-scrolls-what-do-they-prove/.

36 Ralph Earle, *How We Got Our Bible*, quoted in Matthew Trowell, *Who Am I?* (Ontario: Select Media, 2003), 224.

37 "Qumran Cave 1," All about Archaeology, https://www.allaboutarchaeology.org/Qumran-Cave-1-faq.htm.

38 Josh McDowell, *The New Evidence That Demands a Verdict* (Nashville: Thomas Nelson, 1999).
Josh McDowell and Sean McDowell, PhD, *Evidence That Demands a Verdict*, completely updated and expanded ed. (Nashville: Thomas Nelson, 2017).

39 *Merriam-Webster*, s.v. "atone."

40 "Sin," Bible Study Tools, https://www.biblestudytools.com/dictionary/sin/.

41 Eldon D. Enger and Bradley F. Smith, *Environmental Science: A Study of Interrelationships*, 12th ed. (New York: McGraw Hill, 2009), 66.

42 Anthony Campbell, "Thomas Nagel and the Fear of Religion," Anthony Campbell website, rev. September 3, 2017, http://www.acampbell.uk/essays/skeptic/nagel.html.

43 Wikipedia, s.v. "*Mind and Cosmos*," last modified August 2, 2018, 06:27, http://en.wikipedia.org/wiki/Mind_and_Cosmos.

44 *Real Time with Bill Maher*, Season 15, Episode 23, Los Angeles: HBO, August 11, 2017.

45 Quoted on Goodreads, https://www.goodreads.com/quotes/9131099-to-continue-in-atheism-i-would-need-to-believe-that.

www.ingramcontent.com/pod-product-compliance
Lightning Source LLC
Chambersburg PA
CBHW050324120526
44592CB00014B/2040